Manners That Sell

Adding the Polish That Builds Profits

Manners That Sell

Adding the Polish That Builds Profits

Lydia Ramsey

Longfellow Press

For information address:
Lydia Ramsey
PO Box 16545
Savannah, GA 31416
Phone: 912.598.9812
Fax: 912.598.0605
Email: etiquette@LydiaRamsey.com

FIRST EDITION

Cover design by: Eliza Holliday

ISBN 0-9670012-0-X

Longfellow Press

Acknowledgements

No one ever writes a book alone although it often feels like a solitary activity. I have numerous family, friends and colleagues who have given me their support, encouragement and expertise throughout this long process. At the top of my list are Dr. Elizabeth Hoit-Thetford of the Georgia Ports Authority and Craig Barrow of Sterne, Agee and Leach Inc. They were the first to see the potential. Without either of them there would be no business, and there would be no book. Without Esther Shaver of E. Shaver, bookseller there would be no wonderful title.

My very special gratitude to Dr. Lynda Falkenstein, author of *NICHECRAFT: Using Your Specialness to Focus Your Business, Corner Your Market, and Make Customers Seek You Out* for her guidance and cheerleading from start to finish; to Ann Marie Sabath of At Ease Inc. for her willingness to share her ideas and experience; to my dear friend Lucie, who listened to me talk about it for a year and a half; to my daughters, Lauren and Linda, who have always been the greatest believers; and to my husband, "Hank," who generously gave up more than either of us expected so that I could spend hours, days and months in the company of my computer.

To my father, Hoke Wammock, who was the definition of class and will be my model forever.

How To
Use This Book

This book is divided into twelve chapters with each one addressing a key aspect of business etiquette. It is written for those people who are currently in the workplace and who want to promote themselves, their company or organization, their products or their services. It is also designed for those who are preparing themselves to enter the world of work. It is meant to be a guide and reference for appropriate business behavior. For that reason I have allowed room throughout the book for your personal notes. Use this space to jot down ideas for how to apply the information you learn, to remind yourself of behaviors you want to enhance or to list areas that you would like to investigate further. Whenever you have questions that need clarification, call our business etiquette hotline at 800-234-9580 or send us an email at etiquette@lydiaramsey.com. We are always available to assist you with manners that sell.

Foreword

What a treasure this marvelous book is! In all of my business experience I have learned that manners make the sales difference, creating defeat or triumph. I remember my grandmother telling me, *"Politeness is to do and say the kindest thing in the kindest way."*

Manners mean you think of the other person first, what they want, what they need, what would solve their problem, and how you can be of service to them. I have never met a successful business person who did not practice this philosophy.

Recently a client of mine sent me the difference, according to the dictionary, between the words customer and client. He said, "A customer is someone who may wander in, buy something, and you may never see that person again. However, a client is someone who depends on your advice, caring, and continual service. Clients last. Therefore it behooves all of us to create clients." How do you do this? This brilliant book has the answers in such an interesting format! I could not put it down until I enjoyed and savored every word.

There are many historical incidents in which someone was treated very rudely. The results were amazing for the insulter. Susan B. Anthony was very active in the cause to eliminate slavery in the United States. When she stood up to ask a question at an Abolitionist Convention, the chairman told her to sit down and shut up; they did not accept questions from a woman. That was the day she began her movement to obtain equality and the vote for women, a movement that is still spreading around the world.

I enjoyed especially in this book the simple, wonderful things all of us can do to make great first impressions. Jacqueline Kennedy Onassis often said, "She hung on the eyes of men." No wonder they all thought she was brilliant! She not only looked beautiful, she listened carefully to what they said. She gave them the gift of her full attention.

The chapter on greetings and introductions, remembering names, and how to handle business cards is so practical. Of course I knew some of them, but we need to be reminded to practice what we know.

I will never forget the day when I first spoke to Dr. Norman Vincent Peale after I heard him speak. I told him how I had started my business on foot, pushing two small children on a baby stroller that kept breaking down. I offered him my business card, trembling that he might turn away, and not take it. Instead he looked in my eyes, took my card in both of his hands, and then carefully placed it in his inside coat pocket. That moment was the beginning of a long friendship. He featured my story in his *Guideposts* magazine and introduced me to Prentice Hall when the manuscript of my first book was ready. Dr. Peale looked through your eyes into your heart. He listened. He cared.

The "Art of Small Talk" section is charming. Lydia reminds me of a quote from James Barrie, the author of *Peter Pan*, about charm. He said, "It is a sort of bloom in a woman. If you have it, you don't need anything else. If you don't have it, it doesn't matter what else you have." Lots to learn here.

There is so much you will enjoy in this book. All the latest electronic etiquette, new ways to do better with your good friend the telephone, and then how to write all kinds of business correspondence. This book makes the perfect gift for each person on your staff, and for your clients. It is a gold mine of great ideas.

When you begin to practice all of these tremendous ideas, your business will automatically grow like the bean bush in *Jack and the Bean Stalk*. But if you do not, you may have some sad consequences. Leland Stanford and his wife called on a big university in Northern California wanting to give a gift of money to erect a building in the name of their beloved son who had just died. The person who spoke to them did not know who they were. He laughed at them and said they obviously had no idea what buildings cost; then he rose and showed them out of his office. You may have heard of the university that couple built, named for its founder Leland Stanford.

The words in this book will inspire you as they have me. Here are two of them I know a bit about. A person with manners is a great persuader. The word persuade comes into English from French and literally means, "Give good advice in advance." The other word is part of the title of this wonderful book, *Manners That SELL*. My dictionary defines someone who sells as someone who serves. Manners help us do this to perfection, turning customers into clients, building our business to the stars.

Dottie Walters, CSP, International Speaker,
Author, & Consultant
President WALTERS INTERNATIONAL
SPEAKERS BUREAU
PO Box 398; Glendora, CA 91740
PH: (626) 335-8069 FAX: (626) 335-6127
E-mail: Dottie@Walters-Intl.com
Website: www.walters-intl.com

Table of Contents

Chapter Four

Chapter Five

Chapter Six

Chapter Seven

Chapter Eight

Chapter Nine

Chapter Ten

Chapter Eleven

Chapter Twelve

Introduction

Manners matter in the workplace today more than ever. In this highly competitive world where every business has access to technology and information, there is often very little difference in goods and services from one business to another. What sets one organization apart from another and distinguishes one individual from the other are interpersonal skills. Knowing how to treat others with courtesy and respect, being at ease in all situations, and most importantly being able to put other people at ease are the qualities that give people and organizations the competitive edge. Whether you are competing for a client, looking for a new job or seeking a promotion within your organization, your expertise and business ability may not be enough to achieve success if you lack the polish which etiquette provides.

So what is business etiquette? Business etiquette, simply stated, is a set of rules that allow us to interact in a civilized fashion with one another. It is a code of behavior that is grounded in common sense and basic courtesy. Many of the rules of etiquette have been around for centuries, and others are the result of recent lifestyle changes.

This book is devoted to *business etiquette*, not social etiquette, but the two overlap, and the basis for business etiquette lies in knowing appropriate social behavior and applying it to the workplace. Since much of our business life spills over into our social lives and vice versa, the two cannot be completely separated.

There is definitely a renewed interest in business etiquette brought about by a number of significant changes in the workplace within the last two decades. The most obvious of these is the increased presence of women in the workforce. Because men and women are treated equally in business — or so we like to think — many of the rules governing etiquette have had to be revised. Rank is the key to business manners, not age and gender which dictate much of our social behavior.

There is an informality in business which has generated a new set of questions about what is appropriate and what is not. The relaxing of dress codes with the introduction of business casual has created as many problems as it may have solved. Is it business as usual when half the office looks like they came dressed for yard work? The use of first names and the dropping of titles is another example of our current informality in business. Are we being disrespectful or a member of the team when we call the boss by his first name? Does it make her more accessible if we call the CEO "Mary" instead of "Ms. Brown"?

As we experience the phenomenon of the shrinking globe and our business relations take us around the world, we are aware that the rules of business etiquette are different from country to country. We are also finding that for the most part, business people around the world are more formal in their behavior than we North Americans. We understand that in order to be successful globally, we must follow the rule of manners of the host country and be sensitive to the traditions of our international clients.

Who is not aware of the emphasis on diversity in the workplace? We tend to think in terms of racial, ethnic, and religious diversity which have brought about change in the business world. There is another dimension to diversity as a result of the Americans with Disabilities Act. The passage of this act has opened the way for people with disabilities to join the workforce. Their presence challenges many of our old behaviors and requires a sensitivity that was often lacking in the past.

No discussion of workplace changes would be complete without recognizing the effect of technology on business manners. Entire chapters have been added to books on business etiquette in order to deal with fax machines, voice mail and cellular phones. The chapters on business correspondence are being rewritten because of the reliance on electronic mail for both internal and external communications. The term "netiquette" has been coined to cover the rules of etiquette on the Internet.

No wonder there are so many questions about business etiquette today. We are in the midst of tremendous change. The purpose of this book is to eliminate the uncertainty about what is correct in business and to reaffirm the belief that manners are vital to both personal and professional success. Those who read it and incorporate it into their daily business life will become more at ease and confident in their relationships with customers and colleagues. This added polish will be reflected in their profits.

Chapter One

FIRST IMPRESSIONS

First impressions in business are critical to the success of individuals and organizations. That first impression may make the difference in whether or not you form a positive relationship with a potential customer, manage to obtain a sought-after interview, land the contract or get the job of your dreams. We all know the cliches — you only get one chance to make a first impression and it takes a few seconds to make a negative impression and a lifetime to overcome one. In the business arena you may not get the opportunity to make a second impression if your first encounter goes badly. This may not seem fair, but neither is life. Since you can never be sure when and where you will meet a potential client, a possible employer, or a future business associate, you always want to be prepared to make a positive and a powerful impression.

Meeting someone for the first time is like stepping into the spotlight. Everything about you is intensified. Studies show that 55% of how people judge you is based on what they see, 7% is based on the words they hear, and 38% on tone of voice.

The Way You Look

We like to think that you can't judge a book by its cover, but people will judge you first by what they see. Before you ever open your mouth, you create an impression of yourself in the other person's mind. You need to be impeccably groomed and look your best at all times. The day that you decide to dress down or compromise your appearance may be the day that you are introduced to that all-important person whom you have been trying to meet for months.

< Hair >
People focus on your head, face and shoulders first. Whether you are a man or a woman, your hair should be well maintained and well groomed. Extreme hair styles, particularly long hair, do not work well in business. If you choose to have long hair, pull it back or up for work. Hair that is more than shoulder length is often seen as less professional.

< Make-up >
The make-up you wear and how you apply it are critical. It should be done skillfully and in moderation. If you do not feel that you have the expertise to put on make-up correctly, there are numerous sources of help for you. Most beauty salons today have make-up artists, and every cosmetic line has personnel to show you how to apply their products. There are professionals who are available and willing to lend you their expertise, particularly in return for a good customer. Very few women can afford to venture forth without any make-up. With rare exceptions, women who choose not to wear make-up are seen as plain and uninteresting. For those of us who recognize the value of make-up, the trick is to avoid looking like the Painted Desert behind the desk.

< Face >

Facial hair should be well kept. The unshaven look may have appeal in the movies, but in the world of business, it doesn't work. It is hard to have confidence in your banker if he has 5 o'clock shadow at ten o'clock in the morning. Men who choose to have mustaches and beards need to be especially carefully to keep them neat, trimmed and free from unidentified foreign objects.

< Collars >

Shirt collars should be in good condition, and ties correctly tied. The person to whom you are speaking will naturally look at your neck and collar so leave the shirts with the frayed collars for wearing around the house on weekends. Remember to keep your top button buttoned and your tie tied while at work. This doesn't mean that you can never loosen your tie while at work. Just take care to put yourself back in business form before you receive someone in your office or venture outside.

< Jewelry >

Accessories such as scarves and jewelry should also be businesslike. Earrings and necklaces will send a quick message to the person you just met. Save the dangling earrings for evenings and weekends and choose smaller, conservative accessories for the office. It is hard for people to concentrate on what you are saying if your jewelry is the equivalent of a sideshow.

< Shoes >

The next place people look is at your feet. Your shoes send an instant message about you. Believe it or not, people will look at your feet and judge you by the condition of your shoes. They should be polished and in good condition for the workplace. If you look at your shoes and think that it's time to buy new ones, do it. Leave the old worn-out pair at home. If your shoes are in poor shape, you will be judged as someone who doesn't pay attention to detail.

<   Socks   >

Don't take your socks lightly. When people look at your shoes, they also notice your socks. The first thing here is to be sure that they match — not only what you are wearing but also each other! Socks should cover a man's calves. No one wants to look at hairy legs in the midst of business negotiations.

<   Hosiery   >

Stockings are more important than some of us wish to acknowledge. In these days of global warming, women use rising temperatures as an excuse for leaving off the stockings. If getting the job, moving up the corporate ladder or closing the deal are not important to you, go with the bare leg. However, if you want to be successful in the business world, enduring pantyhose is worth the pain. I personally know of an instance where two women were being interviewed for the same job. The interviewers rated them alike in all categories. At the final interview, an outside manager was brought in to help with the difficult decision. He favored one candidate over the other. When asked why, it was because she had worn stockings and the other had not. The woman who wore the stockings got the job because she paid attention to detail, and recognized the importance of the finished look.

Your Body Language

Your body language contributes to the impression you make. Having good posture and walking with authority send a positive message to others. If you look and act confident, people will believe it. So when Mom said, "Stand up straight," she knew what she was talking about.

<   Walking   >

People who walk fast are perceived as more authoritative and efficient than those who walk at a slower pace. I worked with a man whose normal walking speed was almost a run. He was impossible to keep up with. No one was ever quite sure what he did, but he always looked extremely busy and impressive at his fast pace. He also moved just as quickly up the corporate ladder and stayed there while others who were more laid back got left behind or made it up only a few rungs.

<   Eye Contact   >

Eye contact and a smile are essential to a positive impression. It has been said that the eyes are the mirrors of the soul. While you may not want everyone you meet to see into your soul, you want to make direct eye contact during all personal encounters. Looking at others says that you are paying attention and are interested in what they are saying. Maintain eye contact between 50% and 60% of the time. More than that will make the other person uncomfortable and any less will make you appear disinterested or ill at ease.

<   A Smile   >

The impact of a smile is often overlooked. When we first meet other people, we are so busy trying to do and say the right thing that we sometimes forget about our facial expression. A smile on your face can make all the difference in the world. It relaxes the other person, and it says that you are a friendly and confident person. All the well-heeled shoes and designer clothes can never make up for a tense or unhappy facial expression.

< Hands >

Finally, pay attention to where you put your hands. Other people do. Hands belong out in the open in business. Hands placed where they can be seen signal openness and trust. Avoid putting your hands above your neck, in your pockets, behind your back, under the table, or on other people.

Don't put your hands on your face, rub your eyes, or fiddle with your hair. This is a real turn-off because it makes you appear nervous or uneasy. Putting your hands behind your back suggests that you have something to hide or are ill at ease. Let your hands rest at your side when standing and talking to people. While most of us aren't comfortable with our hands in this position, practice doing it and eventually it will become natural.

If it seems awkward having your hands out in the open or by your side, try holding a pen or a pair of glasses in your hand while you are talking.

Standing with your hands in your pockets can send two very contrasting messages. Some people interpret that look as one of arrogance. Others may see you as intimidated or lacking confidence.

Forget what your mother said about keeping your hands in your lap. At business meals and business meetings, hands belong on the table where they can be seen. Rest your hands at wrist level, or slightly above the wrists. Elbows and arms do not belong on the table while there is food on it. In the words of Mae West, "No uncooked joints on the table, please."

Hands never belong on other people. There is only one appropriate touch in the workplace — the handshake. No matter how well intentioned, a pat on the shoulder or a touch on the arm can be misunderstood.

Your Words and Your Tone of Voice

While appearance carries the most weight in creating a powerful impression during face to face encounters, consider the impact of your words and the tone of your voice. In most instances, what we say is not always as important as the way we say it. Pay attention to the tone and quality of your voice. Lower voice tones sound more businesslike and authoritative. A high pitch is a definite turn-off. Seek a voice coach if you have doubts about the quality of your speech. It will be worth the effort to have professional training.

You can sabotage yourself quickly by using poor grammar and vocabulary. This is not a handbook on English grammar, but some people seriously need one. There seems to be an entire generation that missed out on the basics of our language. If you are among those who don't know the difference between certain commonly misused words such as "lie/lay," "sit/set," "rise/raise," "who/whom," and "than/then," to name but a few, *then* I suggest that rather *than* continue in ignorance, you either buy yourself a good book or audio tape on grammar or sign up for a course at your local college or university. The return on investment will be well worth it. Don't let poor grammar ruin your professional image.

> **Avoid unprofessional phrases such as "you know," "you see," "you know what I mean," and today's all-time favorite "you guys." Poor speech indicates a lack of polish.**

Your Notes Here

Your Notes Here

Chapter Two

GREETINGS & INTRODUCTIONS

The successful business person spends a good portion of the day involved in meeting and greeting other people. Whether it is a first time encounter or a repeated occurrence, the way you handle yourself each time you meet someone will directly affect you and your business.

The Handshake in Business

There is no more important gesture in business than the handshake. In fact, it has been said that the handshake is exchanged more frequently than currency in business. The handshake is the unspoken message that accompanies our words of greeting. A good handshake creates a favorable impression. A poor one will cost you business.

A good handshake should be firm, but not bone-crushing. To give a firm handshake, extend your hand with your fingers together and your thumb up and slightly to the side. This will allow you to make contact with the web of your hand, between the thumb and forefinger, touching the web of the other person's hand. Close your thumb over the other person's hand and squeeze firmly. If you see tears forming, you may be squeezing too hard.

Beware of the fingertip and the glove handshakes. The fingertip handshake where one offers just the tips of the fingers is associated with women. Some women extend their fingertips to avoid seeming aggressive, but in so doing they relinquish authority and confidence. Men will sometimes extend just the fingertips to a woman in deference to her femininity.

The "glove" is the handshake where the other person closes his left hand over your right hand during the shake. This may be fine for the clergy when extending condolences, but it has no place in business since it may be interpreted as intimidating and controlling, or in contrast, as a sign of familiarity.

While shaking hands, step in slightly, smile, make eye contact and call the other person by name. The handshake should be accompanied by two quick pumps, which are made from the elbow, not the shoulder. Release the other person's hand after several seconds. Business people are not into holding hands.

If you are seated, stand to shake hands. This applies to women as well as men in business. A woman who remains seated during handshakes and introductions in business gives away her authority and loses credibility.

When should you extend your hand in business? At every opportunity. Extend your hand when:

◊   You meet someone for the first time
◊   You encounter someone you haven't seen for awhile
◊   You greet someone in your office
◊   You see a business associate on the street
◊   You say goodbye
◊   Someone else extends his or her hand

You should not extend your hand when the other person has something in both hands or when the other person has a disability that could make shaking hands difficult. In that case, allow that person to make the first move. We are all familiar with the example of Bob Dole, who shakes with his left hand. If you are not sure which hand to shake or whether it is appropriate to shake at all, wait for signals from the other person.

If someone refuses to shake your hand, don't make an issue of it. The problem belongs to the other person, not you.

Always be ready to shake hands. This means that you should leave your right hand free at all times. Carry briefcases and handbags in your left hand. I recently missed an opportunity to shake hands with a new business contact when exiting an airplane because I was pulling my luggage with my right hand. Pretty unforgivable for a business etiquette consultant!

If you are attending a business/social function, hold your beverage and food in your left hand. You certainly do not want to offer anyone a cold wet hand that has been holding a drink or make the other person wait while you shift objects from one hand to the other.

The handshake is the only appropriate touch in the business world. Hugs and kisses should be reserved for social functions.

If you tend to have sweaty palms, try using an antiperspirant. Since these require about 24 hours to take effect, you should probably apply antiperspirant daily if you have a problem. You might want to keep a tissue or napkin handy for drying your hands. Using your clothing as a towel is not chic.

Managing Introductions

There is good news and bad news about making introductions in business. The bad news is that there are definite rules about making introductions and you need to know them. The good news is that the rules are simple.

Rule #1:

Always make introductions. Have you ever been in a situation where you were not introduced? It's awkward and makes people feel that they are being ignored. Perhaps the person who should be making the introductions thinks you already know the other person. Most likely, that person is suffering from a memory lapse. Whatever the reason, there is no excuse for not introducing people. Everyone feels uncomfortable until introductions are made.

Rule #2:

Introduce the person of lesser authority or importance to the person of greater authority, regardless of gender or age. It is easy to get the order right if you always say the name of the person of greater authority first. For example, you might say, "Mr. Mighty CEO, I would like to introduce Ms. Lowly Manager." or "Mr. Mighty CEO, I would like to introduce to you Ms. Lowly Manager." If you follow this formula, you won't go wrong.

Introductions in business are based on rank and hierarchy, not gender.

Rule #3:

The customer is the most important person. If the president of your company walks into your office while you are talking with a client, you would say, "Ms.

Valuable Customer, I would like to introduce Mr. Mighty CEO, the head of our company." The customer's name is said first.

Rule #4:

Always introduce yourself. Whenever there is the slightest doubt if someone remembers you, introduce yourself. Save others the agony of trying to recall your name. If you are meeting someone for the first time, introduce yourself, giving some information about who you are — not a life history, but a simple statement such as, "Hello, I'm Anne Moore. I represent Great Southern Accents." If you are re-introducing yourself to someone whom you have previously met, mention the connection. "Hello, I'm Anne Moore. We met at the Chamber meeting last month."

Rule #5:

When making introductions, mention some information about the people you are introducing. "Mr. Jones, I'd like to introduce Mr. Smith who is considering moving to our city. Mr. Smith, this is Mr. Jones who is the president of XYZ Bank." This gives the people whom you are introducing the basis for starting a conversation.

Rule #6:

Look directly at people whom you are introducing when you say their name.

Remembering Names

All that is well and good, but now you ask, "What if you can't remember someone's name?" How do you handle this sticky situation? Choking on an hors d'oeuvre and rushing from the room is not a solution. The best approach is to be up front and honest by admitting that you have forgotten the person's name. We have all forgotten someone's name at one time or another. Chances are that you will not offend the person if you explain that you are suffering from a momentary lapse of memory. Some people are very easily offended, but happily there are not as many of them as there are the other kind.

There are a few tricks you can try if you can't remember a person's name, but they are not without risk. If you are standing with two people whom you need to introduce and you can only remember one name, you can try saying, "Do you two know each other?" and pray that they take their cue and introduce themselves. If they reply "No" and look back to you, you are now in trouble.   .

The best technique for remembering names is to repeat the name in conversation as soon as you are introduced.

The best tactic to use when you have forgotten a name is to walk up to the person and introduce yourself. The correct response when people introduce themselves is to give them your name. The risk here is that the other person will say, "Oh yes, I remember you" and stop there.

You can soften the blow of having forgotten a name if you can offer some bit of information that acknowledges the other person and says that you have a clue, but not enough for a name. For instance you might say, "Hello, I'm Anne Moore. I met you at the United Way luncheon last week, but I've forgotten your name." In case the other person can't remember you either, this will help to place you.

Be gracious when you are introduced incorrectly. When someone mispronounces your name or gives the wrong information, make the correction quickly and politely without embarrassing anyone. "My name is Lydia, not Linda," or "I am with Great Southern Accents, not Northern Traditions." This is especially important if you will see this person again, and of course, you never know when and where that may occur.

Exchanging Business Cards

Exchanging business cards is an important aspect of doing business. Your card itself and the way you present it are a part of your professional and personal presence. You want to be sure that your card represents you and your business appropriately. Unless you are in the business of being cute, you don't want a cute card. If your business is professional, your card should look professional.

Your card should be printed on quality paper and include all the necessary information, such as your company name and logo, your name and title, your business address, phone and fax numbers, and your e-mail address and website, if applicable. There is quite a lot of information to be printed on cards today, but I recommend that you stay with the standard 3 1/2 x 2 inch card. While larger cards attract attention initially, they don't fit in most wallets or card cases and so are easily misplaced. If you have more than one business, print separate cards for each.

Use only professional titles such as doctor or professor on your card. You may use degree initials such as Ph.D. or Ed.D. after your name. Do not use Mr., Ms. or another honorific unless your name could be construed as either masculine or feminine. In that case, use the honorific. However, a good way around this dilemma is to print your full middle name. For example, instead of Lee Brown, use Lee Ann Brown. It sounds less pretentious than Ms. Lee Brown, and it makes the point.

A few words of caution: Never leave home or work without your business cards. You never know when opportunity will present itself so follow the Boy Scout motto and always be prepared.

Carry your business cards in an attractive professional-looking case so that they are always in mint condition. You do not want to hand someone a card that looks like you just fished it out from the bottom of your hand bag or the pocket of your wetsuit. When you are attending a business/social function, put a few cards in a convenient pocket (not the one you are sitting on) so that you won't have to dig around for them. You want to be able to produce your card as easily as a magician pulling a rabbit out of a hat.

Present your card so that the person receiving it can read it without having to turn it around. The way you receive a business card also sends a message. Take time to look at the business card when it is given to you and make a comment to acknowledge that you have read it. You might mention the logo or comment on the office location. You'll think of something.

Never present an out of date business card. As soon as any of the information has changed, have new cards printed. You don't want to give someone a card with information crossed out or written over. This is not the place to economize on office supplies.

Never force your card on anyone. Wait for the other person to ask before presenting your card. There are ways to get people to ask for your card. The simplest is to ask other people for theirs. This usually elicits the desired response.

Business cards are a must if you are traveling abroad.

Never ask for a business card during a meal, regardless of whether it is formal or informal. Wait until the meal is over to exchange cards. Of course, if someone asks for your card during a meal, it would be rude to refuse.

Never, never, never exchange business cards at a social function. Doing so will make you look opportunistic and can be insulting to your host or hostess. You will have to rely on memory to make the contact following the event. If that is too scary a thought, one alternative is to carry engraved calling cards with your name and phone number for use at social functions. Another tactic is to have pen and paper handy so that when you leave the function, you can jot down the name of the person whom you have just met.

It is rude to make notes on someone else's business card while that person is present. If you need to remember something about the person, write it on the card after you have parted company. Business cards should not be used for scratch pads.

Your Notes Here

Your Notes Here

Chapter Three

THE ART OF CONVERSATION

While it is important to have good work skills and to be competent in your area of expertise, you will have difficulty being successful if you can't talk to people one on one. People who talk too much are seen as nervous and insecure. Those who talk at the wrong time are viewed as inconsiderate, and those who can only talk about business are boring. People with nothing to say come across as snobbish or aloof.

Many people make the mistake of thinking that being good at conversation means doing all the talking. In fact, being a good conversationalist means listening more than you talk. It is knowing when to talk, when to listen and most especially how to listen. Setting the stage for conversation is a critical first step. To set the tone for conversation and to send the message that you are ready to listen, think about your facial expression, eye contact and body language.

Being a good conversationalist means knowing when to talk and what to talk about. More than that it means encouraging the other person to talk.

A friendly smile sets the tone for good conversation. By smiling when you listen, you send a signal that you are sympathetic and receptive. Many people forget to smile when they are concentrating on listening. They fail to understand that without a smile, they may be perceived as distracted, indifferent or displeased. Remind yourself to smile even when you don't particularly feel like it. Of course, your facial expression needs to be consistent with the message you are hearing. Don't smile if it is not appropriate.

Eye contact is one of the best ways to tell people that you are listening without opening your mouth. In fact, if you are not looking at the speaker, it may be assumed that you are not listening or are not interested in what is being said. Too much eye contact is staring, and makes others uncomfortable. Maintaining eye contact approximately 50-60% of the time offers a good balance between staring and looking uninterested.

Your posture communicates your interest in what the other person is saying and your readiness to listen. Stand with your weight evenly distributed and your feet parallel so that you look like you are ready to listen and not about to bolt from the room. Take care to nod occasionally to confirm your interest. Lean forward slightly, but be careful not to invade the other person's "space." If you notice someone backing up or looking for escape routes, you have probably moved too close.

A comfortable space between people is two to three feet, or the distance of a handshake.

Allow others to speak. This means not interrupting while someone is talking. Too often we are so anxious about what we are going to say next that we fail to let the other person finish. Pause after you think the speaker is through so that you don't talk over what is being said.

> **If you are too busy thinking about what you are going to say next, you aren't listening to what the other person is saying.**

Ask questions based on what you are hearing. This will encourage the speaker and show interest on your part. Open-ended questions that ask for more information will keep the conversation flowing, the speaker speaking, and you looking like a terrific conversationalist.

Use simple confirming phrases, such as "I see" or "How interesting" to indicate that you are paying attention. Another tactic is to paraphrase or repeat what has been said. People are flattered to hear their words repeated.

The Significance of Small Talk

Understanding the value of small talk in business will speed you on your way to success. While it may sound trivial, small talk is the basis for establishing relationships and putting people at ease in business. Engaging in light conversation before a business meeting or meal helps to establish a friendly relationship with clients and colleagues. Small talk may relieve tensions that are building, or simply serve as proof that you are not a total bore who can only discuss work issues.

> **Small talk is an acquired skill which requires a genuine interest in other people.**

Plan in advance for small talk. How often have you been engaged in conversation and wished that you had a script for what to say next or how to respond on a certain subject? Planning ahead can help to avoid those awkward moments. Don't wait until you pick up the client at the airport or meet the new boss for dinner before you think about what you will say.

Find out something about the people you will be meeting. Try to get information about their background and interests so that you are prepared with topics for conversation. If you are not able to find out anything in advance, then think of some general subjects and decide what you will say. Things may not go exactly as you planned, since life seldom does, but at least you will have a start.

Use language everyone understands. Avoid the company jargon if not everyone present works for the company.

Be up-to-date on current affairs. Successfully managing small talk means knowing what is happening in the news. You should read a local newspaper and a national newspaper every day. The more knowledgeable you are on a variety of subjects, the more impressive you will be. In today's high-tech world with Internet access and round-the-clock television news, there is hardly any excuse for not being up-to-date on what is going on around the world.

Know which topics are safe. The weather is always a good subject. Everyone can talk about it, and it changes daily. Other good topics are travel, sports, books, and movies. If the person with whom you are speaking does not show any interest in one subject, be ready to try another. Eleanor Roosevelt used the alphabet as her guide to conversation.

She would start at "A" and work her way through the alphabet until she found a subject that was of interest to the other person.

Knowing what not to talk about is as important as knowing what to talk about. Stay away from controversial political issues and religion. You should also avoid discussing health issues, personal misfortunes, the cost of things, and off-color jokes. If you wonder whether a topic is appropriate or not, it probably is not.

Since the goal of small talk is to build positive relationships in business, keep a check on how interested and involved others are in the subject. The last thing you want to be is boring or offensive. That is another reason for maintaining eye contact during conversation. If you see the other person's eyes start to glaze over, you may want to change the subject or move on.

When to Begin and End Small Talk

Having established the significance of small talk, suitable topics, and techniques for engaging other people, the next step is understanding when it begins and when it ends. Allowing it to continue too long will cause business people to feel that their time is being wasted. Cutting it short can affect the cordial atmosphere of the event whether it is a business meal or a meeting.

Small talk is usually limited to ten or fifteen minutes at lunch and thirty minutes at a dinner meeting. There are variables in every situation. It is best not to begin discussing business until you have ordered your meal so that you won't be interrupted by the waiter in mid-sentence. If people have been in meetings or traveling, they may need a little more time before getting down to business.

The host decides when to end the small talk and begin the business discussion. As the guest, you must allow the host to take the lead even if you are anxious to get down to business. Some people enjoy "chit-chat" more than others.

In a business meeting, small talk should continue long enough to let everyone get settled and acquainted with one another. More than that and people will think that you are wasting their time.

Small Talk in the Office

Small talk in the office is sometimes viewed as meaningless and a waste of valuable work time. Knowing something about the people you work with and being able to talk about issues other than work is often key to establishing a good organizational climate. As long as people remember that by definition small talk is a brief discussion of a relatively neutral and insignificant topic, then it remains useful in the workplace.

The time and the place where small talk is carried on are key. Locations such as workrooms, hallways, and elevators are ideal because there is little chance of disturbing other employees. Certain times of the day lend themselves to small talk. Arrival and departure from the office are times when you are less likely to interrupt someone's work. Just before a meeting is a good time because it helps to set a friendly tone.

Don't let yourself be deceived by the setting. A co-worker waiting for an elevator or walking down a hallway may be concentrating on the business ahead and not be in the mood to carry on a conversation. Don't be offended if a co-worker doesn't greet you every time you pass, or doesn't want to converse at every encounter.

Know when to end the conversation. Small talk is meant to be brief, and the workplace is meant for working. Be careful not to overstay your conversational welcome by talking too long.

Be conscious of the impact of your conversation on others. Be aware that others close by may be disturbed. Speaking in low tones helps but does not always solve that problem. It may even be more distracting.

Keep your small talk to 4-5 minutes. Anything longer than that should be reserved for a break or lunch.

Always stay clear of the office politics and in-house gossip. Avoid talking about your co-workers on a personal level. It is also unwise to engage in speculation and rumors within the organization. Small talk is meant to be impersonal and friendly conversation. If you have issues with the company, take them up with the appropriate people at the appropriate time.

Your Notes Here

Your Notes Here

Chapter Four

DRESSING FOR BUSINESS

The Queen of England is reported to have told Prince Charles, "Dress gives one the outward sign from which people can judge the inward state of mind. One they can see, the other they cannot." Clearly, she was saying what many people are reluctant to accept; that like it or not, people judge us by the way we dress. In all situations, business and social, our outward appearance sends a message. Try going to a busy restaurant at lunchtime. Look around you at what people are wearing and see if you don't make judgments about who they are, their line of business, even their personality and their abilities. Think about how you feel when you are dressed in your usual business attire as opposed to casual dress. Professional appearance translates to professional behavior and credibility. If you wish to promote yourself and your organization, you need to know what constitutes appropriate business dress.

Of course, the industry you are in, the job you have, the geographic area, and the climate in which you work all influence your business attire. People in finance who deal with other people's money are expected to dress conservatively, while those who work in the fashion industry dress to reflect current trends. People who do business in

Miami wear very different fabrics and styles from those worn by people who work in Manhattan. Employees who interact directly with clients must pay close attention to their appearance and how it represents their organization, while those who work behind the scenes can dress more to their own liking.

The most important aspect of dressing for business is knowing what your clients expect to see. They are after all the heart of your business. Customers who see the bank president looking as if he is headed for a day at the links may be somewhat reluctant to entrust him with their hard-earned money. The retail clerk who looks like she dressed at the second hand store will not help to promote the latest fashions. The social worker who is wearing a designer suit will have difficulty communicating with a client who can't pay the rent.

With the relaxation of dress codes, many people are confused about what is appropriate for business and what should be reserved for home. You can enhance your professional appearance by selecting business clothing that is appropriate, attractive, affordable and assured. It should be appropriate for your profession, your geographic region, your job title and the occasion. It should enhance your personal features and should fall within your budget. Finally, your choice of clothing ought to give you a sense of confidence and assurance.

Professional Dress for Women

Women's business dress allows for more self-expression and individuality than men's attire. However, because there are more choices for women, there is also more room for error. Women are challenged to project a professional image while expressing their own personalities and tastes.

The business world is not the place to make strong fashion statements unless, of course, your business is fashion.

Happily, the days when women in business had to dress to look like men have vanished. The severe business suit with its imitation tie is a thing of the past. Women are more confident about their place in the business world, and their choice of professional attire reflects that assurance.

<   Suits   >

The skirted suit is the recommended choice for a career wardrobe. The jacket and matching skirt send the most powerful message with the next option being the skirt and jacket in contrasting or coordinating fabric or color.

<   Jackets   >

Jackets test best for business. There are a variety of jacket styles to choose from that will add a professional look to pants, skirts and dresses and that will flatter different body types. The tailored lapel jacket or blazer is classically correct and, when chosen in a solid color, offers flexibility to a wardrobe.

<   Dresses   >

Dresses that work well are the simple coatdress or the shirtwaist because of their tailored look. If you choose to wear a dress, put a jacket with it for more authority.

A bit of lace or eyelet trim is acceptable but the frilly look is not professional.

< Pants >

Pants, when they are part of a matching trouser-and-jacket suit, are being worn more and more frequently by business women. However, the pants suit is still seen as less conservative than the skirted suit and should be worn with caution if you are trying to achieve the executive look.

< Blouses >

Tailored blouses and fine-gauge sweaters work well for business. Blouses are a good place to add personality and color to your wardrobe. Most fabrics are suitable unless they wrinkle excessively or are of the see-through variety.

< Fabrics >

The recommended fabrics for women's clothing are 100% wool, wool blends, silk, cotton and linen. Beware of some cottons and linens, which by 10 a.m. can look like you slept in them the night before. The new micro-fibers are easy to care for, look very professional and maintain their quality of appearance after a long day at the office. They are not the same as, nor do they look like, the polyester of the 70's.

The secret to the professional look is to go with solid colors and muted prints and to avoid floral or bold patterns.

< Colors >

In choosing colors for business, again there is more flexibility for women. Navy, black, brown and taupe, all of which are considered neutral, look very professional and are easy to mix and match to extend your wardrobe. Blouses in virtually every color can add variety to your neutral suits without adding great expense. However, there is no reason for women to avoid color in selecting suits as long as the style conveys a professional look. In fact, according to some image consultants, high contrast combinations of jackets and skirts convey the highest authority.

A good rule to follow is to note how the most senior woman in your organization dresses, then imitate.

<   Shoes   >

The classic leather pump with a closed heel and toe is the shoe of choice in business. Heels should be in a range of 1 to 3 inches. Anything higher than 3 inches is out of place and for most women is just plain uncomfortable. Although real leather shoes cost more, they are worth the investment in durability and appearance.

There is no reason to wear those aerobic shoes to and from the office. Since today's shoes are designed for comfort, style and durability, women do not need to mix their exercise footwear with their executive dress.

Shoes in neutral shades are best: black, gray, navy or taupe. The color of your shoe should match or be darker than your hemline. You never want the style or the color of your shoes to detract from your appearance or to be the focal point of your attire. (Think of the Wicked Witch of the West in The Wizard of Oz. Do you want to be remembered for your red shoes???)

<   Hosiery   >

Neutral-colored stockings are the appropriate look for business. Although a tone which matches your skin is the most conservative, sheer or semi-opaque black and navy stockings work well in your professional wardrobe. Bright colored stockings or patterned ones are not appropriate for business.

<   Handbags   >

Handbags, briefcases, and portfolios should also be of the best quality that you can afford. They should convey a professional look, so avoid carrying a handbag that resembles an overnight bag or a briefcase that is reminiscent of a steamer trunk. Definitely don't carry them both at the same time. A slender or compact handbag is appropriate when carrying a briefcase, but if you can manage to put personal articles in your briefcase and abandon the handbag, you will look more businesslike. It may take some searching, but there are handbags that look like slender briefcases and there are briefcases that pass for handbags. Finding one of these eliminates the confusion of which one or how many to carry.

<   Jewelry   >

Jewelry can add to or detract from your total appearance. The most professional look comes from wearing gold or silver jewelry. If you cannot afford 14 carat gold or sterling silver, choose the best you can. Pearls give a professional look. Avoid wearing oversized or "noisy" jewelry such as large dangle earrings and charm bracelets. Please, only one earring per ear.

Jewelry should be proportional to your size. Tiny dainty earrings on a tall woman reduce her authority. Large earrings on a small woman can make her look all ears.

Rings should be limited — one to a hand. You can forget wearing more than one ring per finger if you want to appear professional. Avoid wearing a large ring on your right hand because it could inflict pain on you or the other person while shaking hands.

The watch you wear to work should be of good quality and businesslike in appearance. Reserve fun watches for weekends.

Professional Dress for Men

Men have fewer wardrobe choices than women, but this doesn't mean that dressing for business is a "no-brainer." They need to work a little bit harder on the subtle variations that can lend personality, style and taste to their appearance. Basically, men have two choices in business attire: the two-pieced suit or the sport coat and trousers. As usual, the decision about how to dress should be made based on the company you work for, the job you hold and the area of the country where you work. When in doubt, check how upper managers are dressed. Let those with proven track records influence your decision.

Both men and women should dress for the job they want, not the job they have.

<   Suits   >

The two-pieced suit is usually the best choice in business. Choose suits in gray, navy or charcoal. Some browns and black can create a negative reaction. Solids are safest, but muted plaids and pinstripes are also acceptable.

As for style, while the single-breasted jacket works best, double-breasted jackets are popular in certain regions. Double-breasted jackets are always buttoned, including the inside button. It is a good idea to check out the rear view in a mirror to be sure that your jacket hangs straight when buttoned. If it doesn't, find the size that does.

A sport coat and trousers convey a more casual look and are perfectly acceptable in less formal business environments. However, jacket and pants should be a clear contrast. Avoid plaid coats because of their overly casual look.

< Colors >

The colors that work best in business are much the same for suits as for sport jackets and pants. Brown and camel, however, are acceptable for jackets, and pants can be a lighter shade, such as tan or beige, when worn with darker jackets.

< Fabrics >

Fabrics that are best for both suits and sport jackets are wool and wool blends. Wool blends can be worn virtually year round and resist wrinkling. That's always a plus. Silks and silk blends are also good for suits.

< Shirts >

Shirts in business should always be long-sleeved, even in summer. Thank heaven for air-conditioning. The best choice in fabric is cotton, which is good news for the summer months. However, cotton does need ironing. Unless you are adept with an iron, have your business shirts done at the laundry. Solid colors are preferred for business shirts, with white being the most tried and true. Light blue also works, but avoid other colors unless your work environment supports a more creative look.

< Ties >

Ties can add personality and pizzazz to your business suits, but because there are more choices in this category, there are more cautions. Ties should complement your suit or jacket, not match.

While the width of your tie is dictated by current fashion, as a rule ties should be approximately three inches wide and should reach the top of your belt buckle.

While a wide range of patterns and colors are available, stay away from ties that are loud or wild. Those goofy ones with the Disney characters should be saved for the company party. Small geometric prints and stripes are good, as are paisley patterns. Silk is the best fabric for ties. It is always appropriate with whatever you wear and whatever the time of year.

< Belts >

Belts should be of good quality leather or reptile skin and should match your shoes. If you prefer, you may wear suspenders or "braces," but don't wear a belt and suspenders. It is a sure sign of paranoia.

< Shoes >

People will notice your shoes. So, again, choose the best quality that you can afford. Lace-up or slip-on styles are better in business than tasseled loafers, which are a little too casual. Always wear shoes that are as dark as or darker than your trousers. Check regularly for run-down heels and scuffed toes. Repair them before the need becomes obvious to everyone.

Your socks need to cover your calves and match or blend with your trousers. And of course they should always match each other.

Men's jewelry should be limited to one ring per hand and a good quality watch. It's that simple.

The New Business Casual

Nothing has generated more discussion or caused more confusion in the workplace than the advent of business casual. Dress-down or casual days are adored by some and abhorred by others. Few companies seem to have a firm idea of what it means, and even fewer employees understand what is appropriate and what is not under the new rules. The difficulty comes primarily when businesses decide to institute a dress-down day without putting in place a clear and detailed policy.

Most people credit Silicon Valley for the gift of business casual. In the 1980's these youthful geniuses saw no reason to conform to business tradition. These were the folks who understood Pentium chips but couldn't operate the household iron. The idea was quickly embraced by the generation that had gone off to college with blue jeans and tee shirts as the mainstay of their wardrobe.

Some people like the idea as the great equalizer in the workplace. On dress-down day, supposedly the CEO and the frontline worker are indistinguishable. Where has that ever been true? Others have adopted the idea because employees said that they could be more productive if they were dressed comfortably. The debate over this practice rages on. While there are companies who report that productivity is up because employees are more comfortable, there are those who find that when their employees dress less professionally, they behave less professionally.

At the risk of oversimplifying a complex issue, it seems that there are two key elements to the success of business casual. The first is having a clear policy on casual dress for your business. Left to their own devices, employees can come up with any number of creative ways to dress for work.

Every organization should have their written dress code policy clearly communicated to all employees.

The second is knowing what is appropriate casual dress for your specific organization, particularly with regard to your clients and the outside world. Most large department stores used to have very strict dress codes, some so rigid that it was hard to tell by the way the clerk was dressed if you were shopping for a cocktail dress or a casket. Today the issue is trying to figure out who the salespeople are. Many of them are so under-dressed that they are indistinguishable from the crowd lined up to run in the Boston Marathon.

There are businesses that haven't figured out that their standard of dress is already so relaxed that a dress-down day makes no sense. If your usual business attire is suits or sport coats and jackets for men and skirted suits and dresses for women, there may be some benefit from a casual day. Otherwise, what's the point?

What is the "real" definition of business casual? According to Ann Marie Sabath, Author of *Beyond Business Casual: What to Wear to Work if You Want to Get Ahead,* the real definition of business casual is to dress down one notch from what you would normally wear for business professional. That is, if you usually wear a suit and tie to work, dressing down means that you would wear a sport coat and trousers. If a sport coat and trousers are your normal attire; you might leave off the tie. To go a notch further, wear a polo shirt with your trousers. For women, you may choose to go to the office in a quality pants suit instead of your usual skirted suit. If your regular attire is a skirt and coordinating jacket, you may choose to wear pants instead.

If you have to apologize to your customers or explain what you are wearing, then you made the wrong decision when you got dressed.

Business casual does not mean throwing all caution to the winds and wearing your favorite old clothes to the office. The operative word in the phrase "business casual" is "business." You always want to look as if you are prepared to do business.

What should you avoid wearing on casual day?
- ◊ Torn or wrinkled blue jeans
- ◊ Sweat pants or jogging pants
- ◊ Leggings or Spandex pants
- ◊ Shorts of any kind
- ◊ Ultra-short skirts
- ◊ T-shirts with logos
- ◊ Clothing with printed slogans
- ◊ Tank tops
- ◊ Cropped tops
- ◊ Sweatshirts
- ◊ See-through blouses
- ◊ Sandals
- ◊ Hiking boots
- ◊ Dirty old tennis shoes

Know when *not* to wear business casual. Just because it is casual day at the office, don't make the mistake of dressing down if it is not appropriate for the events of the day. Check your calendar before you get dressed. Don't jeopardize yourself or your organization with your attire.

When should you avoid business casual? When ...
◊ You have meetings or luncheons outside the office
◊ You are in negotiations
◊ You are expecting a client in your office
◊ You are dealing with an international client
◊ You are in doubt about the appropriateness of your clothes
◊ Your performance review is scheduled for that day

Two words of caution:
1. Even if you are not in agreement with the concept of business casual, don't avoid it altogether. If you do, you may be viewed as someone who is not part of the team or cannot adapt to new ideas.
2. Women should not dress down as much as men. An executive male still looks like an executive male in his casual clothes. A female executive tends to look like a lower ranking person when she dresses down. For that reason, even if blue jeans are acceptable on a casual day, women should avoid them and go with more tailored and fitted casual clothes. A woman's credibility is still very much connected to her professional clothing. As appealing as casual days are, we all should remember that dressing up to go to work is a discipline that reflects a respect for your organization and your clients as well as for your own hard-earned professional skills.

Your Notes Here

Your Notes Here

Chapter Five

TELEPHONE COURTESY

Seventy-five to eighty percent of all business is conducted over the phone today. Every ring means business, and every phone contact is the opportunity to build customer relations. By the same token, a single phone conversation handled improperly can result in not just one lost customer, but several potential customers as well. Bad news travels faster than good news so unhappy callers will not keep the negative experience to themselves. They will tell someone else for sure, and chances are they'll tell more than one.

The telephone may be the first and only contact you have with a customer. Make it your best.

Every businessperson needs to practice good telephone skills. This means knowing how to receive calls and how to place them. It means understanding how to manage all the telephone options available today, including answering machines, voicemail, cellular phones, and speakerphones. You can build your business and enhance your professional reputation by handling phone communication politely and efficiently.

It's Not What You Say;
It's The Way That You Say it.

When you meet someone face to face, your tone of voice counts for 35% of the impression you make and your words add up to 7%. When you meet someone over the phone, your tone of voice soars to 70% of the impression you make and your words to 30%. Callers have no idea how good your hair looks, how well you applied your make-up or how professional your attire is. They can only judge you by what they hear. Your words are important, but we all know that you can say, "Have a nice day" and sound like you mean well, or you can say "Have a nice day" and your words become a threat.

Give the caller your full attention. It is not hard to tell when people are paying attention or when they are distracted by something else that is going on.

The beauty of the telephone is its availability. With cellular phones today, we have to do little more than reach into a handbag, briefcase or pocket to find a phone. Talk about instant gratification! However, what is a marvelous convenience to the caller may be an intrusion to the person on the other end of the line. We never know if the person we are calling is in the midst of an important project, facing a critical deadline or has twelve people lined up waiting for service. The caller has no idea what is going on, and doesn't need to. The person calling only knows that the one answering the phone is friendly, professional and ready to assist. Good telephone manners dictate that no matter what is happening when the phone rings, the caller must feel welcomed and valued.

Answering the Phone

Smile when you answer the phone. Regardless of what is going on around you, put a smile on your face and in your voice. Although your caller cannot see you, the smile is reflected in your voice. Keep a mirror by your desk so you can see yourself as others hear you. (Share this tip with your co-workers so they won't think you have suddenly become enchanted with your own good looks.) You will come across as friendly and helpful when you smile into your phone.

Answer the phone before the second ring and no later than the third. In today's instant world where we stand in front of the microwave saying, "Hurry up," no one expects to wait for long. If you don't answer your phone quickly, people are likely to decide that you are not very efficient and take their business elsewhere.

Greet your caller with a professional "Hello" or "Good Morning" followed by the name of your organization and your name. Give both your first and last name when answering the phone. Unless you intentionally want to convey an informal business atmosphere, your caller should hear both names. "Hello. This is Mary Smith" sounds more professional than "Hello. This is Mary."

Your telephone greeting is the equivalent to your verbal handshake and introduction.

Avoid eating and drinking when you are on the phone. You may think that the caller cannot hear you, but those sounds are magnified. You wouldn't continue eating if someone walked into your office, so don't do it in front of a caller.

If you are talking to someone in your office when the phone rings, excuse yourself to answer the phone. Don't pick up the phone and continue to talk to the person in your office. If you need to finish the conversation with your office visitor after you have answered the phone, ask permission to put the caller on hold or to return the call.

Ask someone else to take calls or use your voice mail when you are meeting with someone in your office. A visitor with an appointment in your office has priority over a phone caller. If you are expecting an important call when someone drops by your office, let your office guest know that you may need to interrupt the visit to answer the phone.

Placing Callers on Hold

Ask permission before putting someone on hold. That doesn't mean answering the phone by saying pleasantly, "Good Morning XYZ Company, Mary Smith speaking. May I ask you to hold please?" and instantaneously pushing the hold button. Wait until callers give you permission before placing them on hold. It is just plain rude to ask the question and not wait to hear the response. The caller may prefer to call back or may not be in a position to hold for an undetermined amount of time. Placing someone on hold without getting permission is tantamount to hanging up on that person.

Consider the language you use when placing someone on hold. It doesn't sound very professional to say, "Hang on." This conjures up images of Harrison Ford hanging on to the tail section of Air Force One. Instead, ask your caller, "May I put you on hold for a moment please?"

The person on the line has priority over an incoming call. If you have to answer another line, take a message from the second person and return to the original caller immediately.

Return to the call within 30-60 seconds. Waiting time always seems longer to the person on hold. If necessary come back on the line to ask permission to extend the hold period. You don't want your callers to feel that they have been placed on eternal hold never to hear a human voice again. When you get back to the caller, be sure to say, "Thank you for holding."

Ask permission to call people back if you know that they will have to hold for longer than a minute or two. Be honest about the length of the wait. People like to have choices and will be impressed with your consideration.

Taking Messages

If you are taking a message, be sure to get all the necessary information as accurately as possible. Take down everything that the person returning the call will need to know. Get a phone number even when the caller says, "Oh, I'm sure that Mr. X has my number." This may not be the case, and you will save the other person precious time looking up the number. Verify the name of the caller, asking for correct spelling if necessary. Finally, read back the message to be sure that you have it right. The caller will be grateful for your extra effort.

If voice mail is available, you may want to suggest putting the caller through to a voice mail box. Leaving a message on voice mail assures that the information left is accurate. Once again, always ask permission first. Some people have a serious aversion to voice mail and prefer to leave the message with a living, breathing person in spite of the risks involved.

Transferring Calls

If you are transferring a call, advise the caller that you are doing so. Give the person the extension to which you are transferring the call in case the call is disconnected. Before you transfer the call, inform the person to whom you are making the transfer about the caller and the nature of the call. This will save the caller from having to go through the same story several more times, depending on how many times the person has already been transferred or had to call back.

Always allow the caller to end the conversation. Wait until you hear the person who called say good-bye and hang up before you replace the receiver. Don't risk hanging up on your caller or appearing eager to get off the phone.

Making Phone Calls

When you are the caller, keep in mind that good manners and good business dictate that you make your call as convenient and as efficient as possible. While the person at the other end of the line hopefully is delighted to hear from you, a phone call is an interruption. Everyone is always doing something else when the phone rings.

Place calls yourself. People who have a secretary initiate their calls send a message that they are somehow more important and their time more valuable than everyone else's. This tactic will not win you friends or influence people.

Identify yourself immediately by giving your full name and the name of your company. "This is Martha Wolf of XYZ Company. May I speak to Ms. Brown?" Say your name slowly and distinctly so the person answering the phone can understand you. Even if you are known to the person you are calling, don't assume that your voice will be recognized or that you need to only say your first name. Avoid an awkward moment by giving your full name and the organization you represent. Think of it as an opportunity for some personal marketing.

> **State at the outset the reason for your call. Don't make a busy person guess what's on your mind.**

Ask if you are calling at a convenient time. People often overlook this thoughtful question and begin talking immediately. Recognize that the other person you are calling has a life, too, and that your call may be an intrusion. If you frequently do phone business with the same person, ask the most convenient time to call. People will appreciate your showing consideration and will use this as reason for doing business with you.

> **When a call is disconnected, the person who placed the call initiates the reconnect.**

Leaving Messages

When you have to leave a message, give all the information necessary for calling you back. Leave your phone number no matter how often the person calls you. The person you are calling may have to return the call from somewhere other than the office where your number is on file. Saving someone else time is always a good move.

Another time-saving tactic is leaving enough information so the other person understands the purpose of your call and is ready with the necessary information when you finally connect.

Be prepared. You never want to waste your time or someone else's, and you always want to come across as professional. Before you place a call, have on hand all the information you need for doing business. If you have a lot to discuss, consider writing down the points you need to cover. That way if you have to leave a message, it will be complete and concise.

Telephone Tag

Telephone tag has become a national pastime. Some of us are better at playing it than others. If you want to improve your game, here are a few simple rules.

Always leave a complete message which includes your name, the company name, and your phone number. Say when you may be reached. Don't ask someone to call you back when you know that you will be out for the rest of the day. Instead suggest times when you will be available. When leaving your phone number, say it slowly so the other person does not have to replay your message several times.

Give permission for the other person to leave you a voice mail or to leave a message with a particular person if you cannot be reached. If you are having difficulty reaching someone, ask that person to leave you a message with a convenient time for you to call back.

When you leave your phone number, give the last four digits in pairs; for example, "My number is 555 ninety-eight twelve." This helps to prevent transposing numbers.

Screening Phone Calls

While most of us agree that screening phone calls is sometimes necessary, it can be overdone. Unless you hold a high political office, are the CEO of a Fortune 500 company or enjoy celebrity status, having your calls screened can come across as arrogant and aloof or just plain customer-unfriendly. None of us wants to place a call, be asked our name and then be told that the person we wish to speak to is "not available." Here are some suggestions for handling this issue whether you are the person making the call, the one receiving the call or the one caught in the middle screening the call.

When you are the person making the call, identify yourself immediately and explain why you are calling. You will enable whoever answers the phone to either put your call through without further questions or to take a message graciously. You will never know if the person whom you are calling is truly unavailable or is just not available to you. You can avoid an awkward moment by saying your name up front.

If you are the person answering the phone and screening calls for someone else, you are often in a difficult spot. If your boss or co-worker does not wish to be disturbed, you need to have some guidelines for what you will say and how you will handle calls. You should first tell the caller the whereabouts of the other person and then ask for identification. "Ms. Smith is out of the office, may I take a message and have her return your call?" Avoid asking someone's name and then saying, "Ms. Smith is in a meeting." This sounds as if Ms. Smith just doesn't want to talk to the person on the line. Don't make the caller feel uncomfortable or unwanted.

Callers only need to know that you are out of the office or unavailable. More information than that can lead to further complications.

If the person for whom you are screening calls wants certain callers put through, you can use the technique of saying up front that the person is in a meeting or not available. Once the caller is identified, you have the option of offering to interrupt the fictitious meeting or trying to locate the person. This allows you to cover most of your bases and avoid placing yourself or the caller in an awkward situation.

Obviously, you can't answer every phone call personally or you would never get anything done. However, if you routinely screen your calls or have someone else do it for you, you may be sending a negative message. Callers are looking for service, and they value accessibility.

All phone calls should be returned within 24-36 hours. If you cannot return calls within that time period, leave a message on your phone to that effect or ask someone else to return calls for you. If you are slow to respond, you may lose a business opportunity.

Conference Calls

Conference calls, which allow a number of people in different locations to be on the phone at the same time, are an efficient and convenient way to conduct business. To be most effective, there are simple guidelines to follow.

◊   Be where you are supposed to be when you are supposed to be there to begin the call. Connecting all parties can be handled in a short period of time if everyone is available at the agreed time and place.

◊ Personal introductions should be made at the beginning of the call. Everyone involved needs to know who is on the line and to hear each voice.

◊ Identify yourself each time you speak. Even if you have spoken several times, don't assume that everyone will recognize your voice or remember who you are.

◊ Use inflection in your voice. The disadvantage of meeting by conference call is that you cannot see the other people or read their body language. By changing the tone of your voice, you can get your point across more effectively and hold people's attention.

◊ Be careful not to interrupt. Wait until you are sure that the other person has finished before you begin speaking. Pauses really are all right although some people get nervous at so much as a hint of silence.

◊ If you are in charge of the call, pay attention to who has spoken and who has not. Everyone should be heard from. Otherwise you might just as well have faxed the information.

◊ During conference calls, use full sentences with descriptive words when you respond. For example, say, "That's a good idea," instead of "Okay." Otherwise, your response may be missed.

Speaker Phones

The speaker phone is another convenience of the modern world, and one that is too often misused and abused. Mention "speaker phone" and you are likely to get a violent reaction from many people.

Never put someone on speaker phone without asking permission first. The proper procedure is to get the person on the line and explain the purpose of your call. Then tell them why you wish to use the speaker phone: "Mr. Brown from our Purchasing Department is in my office, and I would like for him to hear this." Used correctly, this telephone feature can be very beneficial and timesaving. Used incorrectly, it can cause irritation or even embarrassment. There are far too many tales of people speaking candidly about someone whom they did not know was present on speaker phone.

If you are the one who is unwittingly put on speaker phone, you can ignore it or you can explain that you are unable to hear well and ask the other person to use the handset.

Cellular Phones

Cellular telephones have provided us with instant access to people everywhere. There is no reason for anyone to be inaccessible today except by choice. While there are people who have to be available or on call outside of their workplace, there are those who take it too far. When do we cross the line between conducting business appropriately and violating the rules of good manners?

Cell phone ringers should never be turned on in public places. If it is necessary to be reached at all times, carry a beeper — one that vibrates — or a phone that vibrates. It is inconsiderate to have your phone ring in a public place unless you are in the midst of Grand Central Station or a crowded sidewalk where no one will notice. Other people do not need to know how popular or important you are. Having your phone ring in the middle of a meeting, presentation, or concert is annoying and inconsiderate.

Phone calls should be made in private, not in the center of a restaurant, theater or hotel lobby. It is just plain rude to talk on the phone in front of someone else. Excuse yourself and go to a quiet location away from other people to take or return a call. No one should have to listen to someone else's phone conversation. If people choose to conduct telephone business in inappropriate places such as restaurants, waiting rooms, voting lines, and concert halls, it is not just their business. They have made it other people's business.

When it intrudes on the privacy and comfort of others, it is a violation of the rules of etiquette. Anyone who has to talk on the phone in public seems to me to have an ego problem, an excessive case of greed or the world's worst case of time management.

Car Phones

Car phones are now all but standard equipment for automobiles. The rules to observe when using car phones have as much to do with safety as manners.

From a safety standpoint, you should always pull off the road to make a phone call from your automobile. People rarely do this, of course, but most of us have difficulty doing two things at the same time, especially when one of those is driving a car and the other is talking on the phone.

When you are calling someone else's car phone, the first rule of etiquette is to ask if the person is able to talk to you at that moment or would like to call you back under different conditions. The second rule for calling is to be brief. The receiver is incurring the cost, and it is not inexpensive. Discuss only important issues.

Don't put people on hold when they are calling from a car phone. If you are the caller, mention that you are using a mobile phone so the other person will know to be brief.

When you are on the receiving end, identify yourself when you answer. If you have passengers in the car with you, let the caller know who is present and limit your conversation for the sake of your passenger.

Your Notes Here

Your Notes Here

Your Notes Here

Chapter Six

ELECTRONIC ETIQUETTE

The last decade of the twentieth century brought major changes in the way we communicate and exchange information in business. We can now be in touch instantaneously with clients and colleagues anywhere in the world. Wherever we go from airplanes to hotel lobbies to shopping centers, we are never out of reach. With the conveniences of communication come challenges for using the technology in ways that are appropriate, professional and personal. Voice mail, fax machines and e-mail have had an impact on our ability to "reach out and touch someone" without coming face-to-face. We must use the new high-tech systems to our advantage while maintaining the human touch, which is the cornerstone of our business relationships.

Voice Mail

Voice mail is one of the most effective forms of business communication today. It has improved job productivity by allowing people to leave clear and complete messages for each other at any time. Entire conversations can be conducted without the parties ever speaking directly to each other. The challenge for using voice mail is being efficient and personal at the same time. There are a few simple ways to allow this to happen.

Prepare a personalized and current greeting for your callers. Use your own voice, not the canned version that comes with some voice mail services. It is extremely impressive to change your greeting daily, letting people know your schedule and when you may be reached or will be returning calls for that particular day. If you don't want to record a daily version, then try to change your greeting often enough so that it doesn't become stale.

Give your callers an early means for exiting the system. What is more frustrating than being trapped in voice mail listening to a menu of interminable options? If your callers can be given the choice to speak to a "live" person, let them know that up front. Their second option should be leaving the voice mail message.

Make your voice mail greeting as brief as possible. People in business do not have time to waste. Your clients will soon tire of calling you if they have to listen to every option each time that they dial up.

Let your callers know when you will be returning your calls so that they know when to expect to hear from you. Some business people assure their customers that their calls will be returned by the end of that business day. This is very impressive. Whatever you promise, be sure you deliver.

Answer your phone yourself whenever possible. Voice mail is very helpful when you are working on a project and don't want to be interrupted or when you have someone in your office. However, there is no substitute for the real thing.

Your callers will appreciate your availability and personal attention.

Leave clear and complete messages for other people. Always leave both your first and last names, your phone number with area code if dialing outside your area, and the time when you may reached. If you are calling from another time zone, make that clear as well.

Repeat your phone number and say it slowly enough that the other person can write it down without having to play back your message ten times. Some people seem to slip into fast forward to leave voice mail messages for fear that the machine will cut them off before they finish. So what? If that happens, call back and finish the message. Trust me — the person hearing your message will appreciate your thoughtfulness and persistence.

Beepers

The beeper seems to me to have been the invention of the devil. Of all forms of modern communication, the beeper can be the most offensive. Of course, cell phones are joining the competition and may soon surpass beepers as the rudest form of interruption. Obviously, beepers serve a valuable purpose when people must be instantly accessible. However, there is no reason for anyone to wear anything but a silent beeper in public. If you must check your beeper while in the presence of others, excuse yourself just as you would if answering the phone in your office.

Beepers and cell phones should be seen and not heard. For women who wear beepers and cell phones clipped to their clothing, try not to look like you are undressing when you go for the beeper or the phone.

Fax Finesse

Who could have envisioned just a decade ago that fax machines would be as commonplace as the copy machine? While the new technology can certainly speed the transmission of information, it can just as quickly sour a relationship if used improperly. Make sure that your faxes are working for you and not against you!

Send your faxes when promised. Your credibility suffers if your fax is not received when promised. There was a time when we could blame the postal service for information that arrived late, but those days are gone!

Always include a professional-looking cover sheet. Your cover sheet represents you and your organization the same way that your letterhead does. It offers you one more opportunity to put your best foot forward. For convenience and clarity, the cover should state the recipient's name, phone number, fax number, and department if you are sending to a large organization. It should also include your name, phone number and fax number and indicate the number of pages being sent.

If correction fluid is used, make a copy for faxing since white out appears as a blotch when faxed.

Give your fax the same professional appearance as your other correspondence. Just because it is a fax does not mean that it should be any less professional. Documents should be checked for spelling and grammar like any other written correspondence.

Black ink is the order of the day when faxing. Other ink colors will appear lighter on faxed correspondence and will slow the transmission. Copy documents that are printed in anything but black ink before you send them.

Notify the recipient by phone that a fax has been sent. In many large companies a fax can easily become lost in the system. It could be hours or even days before the fax gets to the intended person. Even in small offices a fax can be overlooked.

Be sensitive about sending more than three or four pages. Unless you have been requested to do so, sending a lengthy document can tie up a fax line unnecessarily. This is particularly important when the phone and fax line are the same. Let the recipient know that you need to send more than a few pages, and ask permission.

E-mail Etiquette

E-mail has become one of the most popular and widely used forms of communication in the business world. There are numerous advantages to e-mail. It is quick, efficient and generally informal. It allows you to communicate with others at any time of the day or night without interrupting them. Its flexibility allows you to send lengthy reports or brief messages.

There are disadvantages to e-mail. One is that it has taken the personal touch out of business relationships. Using electronic mail instead of picking up the phone may save time but it doesn't allow for personal interaction which is so necessary to developing good business relationships. Another disadvantage to e-mail is that it is not private. It can be accessed by people for whom it was not intended and it can never be permanently deleted, at least not yet. Caution is advised when using this form of communication.

Because e-mail is a relatively new form of communication, many people are not clear on how to use it effectively, efficiently and appropriately. As a result, a new set of rules has emerged to deal with this issue.

Netiquette is the new term used to refer to civil behavior on the Internet.

Make sure that your e-mail is as professional as all other correspondence. Just because it is e-mail doesn't mean that your message shouldn't be letter perfect. Check for spelling and grammar as you would with any other written document.

Remember that you will be judged by the quality and style of your correspondence. The form and the tone of your letter should be as professional as anything you send out on company letterhead.

Give your e-mail a personal touch. With any form of written correspondence, it is important that your reader feels that the message is directed personally. Use the recipient's name and the word "you" frequently.

When replying to an e-mail, include the original message or an excerpt from it in your response. This will save both you and the receiver the time of having to search out or recall what was previously said.

Check your e-mail messages frequently. You should do so as often as you check your voice mail. You may not need to respond to all messages immediately, but this allows you to answer the most urgent in a timely manner. Your response time should be the same as for a phone call — within twenty-four to thirty-six hours.

Label your message for subject matter. When a message comes through with a subject line that says "No Subject," why would anyone bother to read it? Treat your e-mail like phone messages. Let the other person know up front why you are communicating.

Limit the length of your message. The point of e-mail is to send brief messages and important documents. A document or report may be long, but your message should save your reader time, not waste it. If the message is lengthy, you may want to consider a phone call or one of those old-fashioned meetings instead.

Don't overlook including your company name, address, phone number, and fax number after your signature. The recipient may wish to contact you by "snail" mail or phone instead of by e-mail reply. Make it as easy as possible. After all, it is hard to do business with someone you can't reach.

Be selective in sending e-mail. If everyone in your address group doesn't need the information, don't send it. Sending frequent and unnecessary e-mail is a waste of other people's time. After a while people may stop reading your e-mail messages.

Be selective about what you send. The Internet has become filled with all sorts of junk mail. Not everyone appreciates your sending the latest jokes. Many businesses are concerned about unnecessary e-mail taking up their employees' time. Be certain that the person to whom you are sending the latest joke wants to receive it and has approval for using the company computer for personal entertainment.

Creating a buddy list online is a pleasant way to stay in touch with friends and associates, but remember, when you catch a buddy online, sending an instant message may be an intrusion.

Be cautious about sending messages that are confidential or discuss sensitive subjects. Confidential information should not be sent by e-mail since it is not secure. Your message could be read by the wrong person or inadvertently forwarded to someone else. Sensitive subjects such as job performance, job loss or other personnel issues are more appropriately conveyed in person.

If you use your office computer to send e-mail to friends, be sure you know what the company policy is regarding personal messages.

Your Notes Here

Your Notes Here

___

Chapter Seven

CORRESPONDENCE IN BUSINESS

Talk about a lost art — it's the art of letter writing. Before we had computers, fax machines, voice mail, answering machines, e-mail and cell phones, people actually took time to write letters. Today the business letter is becoming extinct. Yet there is no better way of building business relationships than through letters. They bring a human touch to our sometimes impersonal business dealings.

Letters may be formal or informal. They may address a variety of situations from confirming a conversation or the results of a meeting to extending congratulations or condolences. Whatever their purpose and whatever their style, letters are a permanent record of our words and an expression of our personality. When to write letters is as important as how to write letters. Selecting the appropriate stationery is as essential to the impression you make as wearing the right business suit.

Key Points about Writing Letters

Write letters in a style that is professional, yet reflects your personality. Write as you would speak. Does anyone you know actually say, "As per our conversation dated January

1st"? Avoid using stiff language that sounds like it came from a 1940's textbook. By all means, keep in mind that this is business and don't go to the other extreme by using language that is too familiar and inappropriate for business. If you would be uncomfortable with anyone except the intended recipient seeing your letter, then it probably is not appropriate for business.

Be concise. While a letter is not the intrusion of a phone call, remember that your reader's time is valuable. Keep your letters brief and to the point. Think about your letter ahead of time and list the key points that you want to make. Edit your letter to remove any unnecessary words or phrases. If at all possible, your business letter should be kept to one page.

Proof your letter carefully for grammar and spelling. If your letter is written on a computer, you probably have a spelling and grammar check. Use it. However, have you noticed that you can't always trust your computer? After all, where did your PC get its degree? Read over your letter after you have used "computer check." It is easier to proof a letter if you let it sit overnight or at least several hours. Of course, having someone else proof for you is better yet.

Check the name and title of the person to whom you are sending the letter. If you have any doubt about the spelling of a person's name, the correct title or whether the person is a Mr., Mrs., or Ms., a quick phone call to that person's business will resolve the issue and avoid offending anyone. Your future relationship with someone can be seriously jeopardized by carelessly addressing your letter.

Avoid using the person's first name until you have personally been asked to do so. We have become very informal in business today, but it is wrong to assume that everyone wants to be called by first name. In the beginning of a business relationship, it is better to err on the side of formality.

If you use a computer to write your letter, format the page to left justification only. Full justification with even columns on both sides is harder to read. It looks less personal and more like a form letter.

Your closing should match your salutation. If you address the letter using the other person's first name only, then close with your first name only. If you write, "Dear Joe," close with "Sincerely, Mary." If the letter is addressed to Mr., Mrs., or Ms., close with both your first and last names. If you address the letter, "Dear Mr. Brown," you would sign it with "Sincerely, Mary Smith."

To end your letter, use closings like "Cordially," "Sincerely," or" Warmly." "Very sincerely" or "Cordially yours" sound old-fashioned and a little bit stiff.

Addressing someone by a first name and signing with your first and last name is disrespectful. If you use an honorific such as "Mr." or "Ms." in the salutation and close with your first name, you appear to be subservient. Should we go over that again?

The keyed signature block has become customary in business because so many people have illegible signatures. Penmanship is another lost art. There is no need to use an honorific in the signature block unless your name could be interpreted as male or female. If that is the case, add Mr., Mrs., or Ms. Don't leave your reader in the dark about either your name or your gender.

To "Key" or Write by Hand

There are few gestures in business more impressive than handwriting a letter or a note. Personally writing your letter says that you value the other person enough to go to some extra trouble. Ironically, it takes less time to write a note by hand than to key one yourself or have someone else do it for you.

What if your handwriting is hard to read? Unless it is totally illegible, it is still preferable to send notes in your own writing. With a little time and effort, most of us can improve our handwriting, regardless of our age.

There are times when writing a letter by hand is optional and there are times when it is mandatory. You should always send a handwritten note when:

◊   Someone has given you a gift
◊   You have been a guest in someone's home
◊   You were a guest at lunch, dinner or a party
◊   Someone has done you a favor
◊   You are replying to an invitation
◊   You are sending condolences
◊   You want to recognize a birth, a marriage, or a graduation
◊   You need to apologize

Front, Back, or Sideways?

When you are writing a note by hand, confusion often arises over which side of the paper to write on and which part of the fold-over note to use.

Don't write on both sides of your letterhead. If you need to use a second sheet, use a blank sheet that matches the letterhead in texture and quality. You may write on both sides of correspondence cards if necessary because they are made of heavier stock.

If you are writing on a fold-over note with a monogram or lettering on the front flap, begin your letter on the inside on the bottom half of the folded note. If you need to continue, turn the note over and finish on the back. If you anticipate that your message will be long, start the note at the top of the page when you open up the fold and continue it on the back.

If there is no monogram on the note, make the topside of the note your first page and the inside bottom part of the fold your second page. If you feel longwinded, start on the topside, open up the note all the way and write from the top down for the second page. Turn the note over to the back if you are still going strong. In this case, it may be better to start over on letter-size paper.

The Color of the Ink

The color of the ink that you use should match your stationery. If the color of your letterhead is black, use black ink. If it is blue, use blue ink. If your letterhead or logo is printed in a bold color, stay with black ink unless you are in a business such as advertising where you want to make a strong statement and attract attention. Save the extraordinary colors for your personal notes.

Use blue ink for your signature if your business letter is keyed in black ink. If signed in black, your signature may appear to have been copied.

Thank-You Notes

Writing thank-you notes in business is one of the smartest moves you can make. Sending a written thank-you whenever anyone has taken more than a few minutes to do something for you is a simple act which can have great rewards.

Make it easy on yourself and the recipient by keeping your notes brief. That's why they are called "notes." A few sentences are all that is necessary to show your appreciation and recognition.

Thank everyone who deserves it. If several people were involved in the event or the gift, thank each one individually. Leaving someone out will only generate ill will, since word gets around pretty quickly, particularly in the office.

Always be prepared. If you keep your stationery in a convenient place in your office, you will be able to respond quickly and impressively when the occasion arises. One executive I know has the envelope prepared and the notepaper out ready to write a thank-you before he leaves the office to meet someone. As soon as he returns, he writes the note and it goes into the mail.

Send your thank-you notes within 24-48 hours; of course, the sooner the better.

Sympathy Notes

Sending a note of condolence to a business associate is a thoughtful gesture and an important part of a relationship. Like thank-you notes, these should always be handwritten and brief. Three to five sentences are all you need to express your feelings. This is certainly a time to avoid clichés in writing.

Sending Holiday Cards

Sending holiday greeting cards is a good way to show appreciation to your clients and business friends. With so many cards to choose from today, it isn't hard to find the right one for each individual.

Choose a card that is appropriate for the person's religious affiliation. If you are not certain about a person's beliefs, there are many cards available that are non-religious in nature. These cards wish others "Happy Holidays," "Season's Greetings," or other generic messages.

Mail your cards so that they arrive on time for the holidays. No one will be impressed with a late card. Using a holiday stamp will reinforce the message that you pay attention to detail.

Signing each card and writing a short personal message adds value. Anyone can send cards with a name imprinted on them or can pay to have it done.

Even if the company name is printed on your cards, you should sign your own name. Use both your first and last names unless you are well known to the recipient. Don't assume everyone knows "Joe" at XYZ Company.

Personally selecting and signing each holiday card sends a message that you are sincere. If signing and addressing those holiday cards is a hassle, try addressing the envelopes before Thanksgiving. Then starting the first of December, write your personal messages and sign your cards. All you have left to do is put them in the mail.

Addressing the Envelope

In addressing correspondence, the use of titles is as important as it is in introductions. However, if you check your business mail, you will no doubt discover that nine out of ten pieces are addressed without the use of a title and without a full or even correct name. If you want to be impressive in business and build your profits, trouble yourself to learn correct names and titles, and then use them when writing to your business associates.

Always use a title such as Mr., Ms., Mrs., or Dr. on the envelope. Too much correspondence is being sent without a title or full name, especially when businesses use mailing labels. Omissions of this sort are signs of carelessness.

A handwritten or keyed address on the envelope is preferable to an address label. Use labels only when you can risk your correspondence being thrown into the nearest trash can. To most people a mailing label says, "Bulk mail. Not important." If you use the new clear labels, the address looks as if it has been keyed onto the envelope.

Use a return address on your envelope. This is particularly important if your return address is not printed on the inside note or letter. The recipient should not have to search out your address to send a reply.

Put your return address on the front of the envelope rather than the back flap. The Postal Service prefers it that way.

Correspondence sent to a business should only be sent to persons who are employed there. It is not correct to send mail to Mr. and Mrs. when Mrs. doesn't work there. If you are sending it to both Mr. and Mrs., mail it to their home.

If you are sending a single piece of correspondence to two persons in an office, list the more senior person first. Each name goes on a different line.

Using Correct Titles

For women in business, Ms. is the correct title to use, regardless of her marital state. If a woman feels strongly about being recognized as Mrs., she will indicate this by the way she signs her letters.

When professional titles are used after a person's name, omit the title before the name. Dr. Susan Smith becomes Susan Smith, M.D. and Dr. Donald Jones is Donald Jones, Ph.D. Likewise, when letters indicating an earned degree are placed after the person's name, the title is dropped. You would write Dr. Harriett Hilton or Harriett Hilton, Ed.D., not Dr. Harriett Hilton, Ed.D.

Titles are part of a person's identity. Everyone should be accorded the respect of having the right one used and used in the proper form.

Generational titles such as Sr., Jr., and III can cause confusion when in fact the intent is to eliminate it. These titles should follow the person's full name. You write James Brown, Jr., and not Jim Brown, Jr., unless it happens that Jim is the full name. A son named for his father uses Jr. If both father and son live in the same town, the father should use Sr. to eliminate confusion. When the father dies, the son retains the Jr. for a short period before dropping it. The third generation with the same name uses III following the name. Sr. and Jr. are separated from the name with a comma. III is not. It is Harrison Harrington, Sr., but Harrison Harrington III. Happily, women don't use generational titles as a rule, so this is not an issue for women in business and one less thing to worry about.

Your Stationery Wardrobe

In your business correspondence, the quality and appearance of the paper that you use is as important as the words that you choose. Your stationery should be of the highest quality that you can afford. Often this is the first contact that your customers have with you. The color of the paper and the ink should be determined by the business that you are in. A conservative business organization should stick to classic white or ecru paper with blue or black ink. If you are in the retail world or perhaps own a marketing firm whose business is to get noticed, you might select bolder colors for both paper and ink.

Your business stationery wardrobe should consist of several different pieces:

◊ Regular letterhead, 8½ x 11 inches, with the company name and logo printed on it as well as the address, phone number, fax number, e-mail address and website.

◊ Monarch sheets, which are 6½ x 8 inches with only the company name imprinted. These are used for more personal notes.

◊ Correspondence cards, usually 4½ x 6½, with just the company name and logo. These are perfect for short notes.

◊ Envelopes which correspond to the size of the letterhead or card. The company name, logo and address should appear on the front of the envelope.

Corporate letterhead should never be used for personal correspondence. You should keep a supply of stationery on hand to use for personal correspondence such as thank-you notes, condolences and congratulations. If you are writing letters or notes on behalf of a community organization such as fundraising or membership letters, you would use personal stationery, not the company letterhead. For these occasions you might use a correspondence card, which is the most versatile, or the Monarch-size paper. Only your name is printed on the card or sheet. The matching envelopes are imprinted with the company address, but not the company name or logo.

For a correspondence which is purely personal, never use the company name and address.

Your Notes Here

Your Notes Here

Chapter Eight

ETIQUETTE IN THE OFFICE

The way you treat visitors to your office and co-workers in shared spaces speaks volumes about your professionalism. After all, the office is where most of us spend the greater part of each day. We develop relationships with clients and colleagues based on how we interact with them in the office setting.

Hosting the Business Caller

Be on time to receive your business caller. That ought to go without saying, but unfortunately many business people are not as considerate as they should be. Keeping your caller waiting, especially if it happens more than once, sends a negative message. Don't be surprised when your guest decides to do business with someone else.

Receiving business callers in your office requires the same courtesy and attention as hosting a guest in your home. Your goal is to make the visitor feel welcome, comfortable and, most of all, important.

If you can't receive your caller on time, go to the reception area yourself to explain the delay. If you are delayed in a meeting or situation that you cannot leave, it is acceptable to send someone else with the message. Business emergencies occur. You can't avoid the unexpected. Make every effort to see that your guest is comfortable while waiting. Offer coffee or a soft drink and something worthwhile to read. Trade journals related to your business or your organization's publications and annual report are good choices. Outdated magazines will not entertain or impress your visitor.

By all means, let your caller know how long you expect to be delayed. People are not very good at waiting in today's fast world, especially for undetermined periods of time.

Be prepared to take your caller's coat or umbrella. If you don't have a coat rack or an umbrella stand in your office, figure out ahead of time how to handle these items. Your guest should not be inconvenienced by trying to keep the wet umbrella off your carpet or balancing a heavy coat on a lap full of papers and reports.

Go to the reception area yourself to escort the visitor to your office. As a second alternative, ask your secretary, assistant, or receptionist to usher your guest in. It is most polite to let your guest walk ahead of you to your office. However, it may be more efficient and less confusing to lead the way. Whatever you do, don't put visitors in the position of having to find their way to your office from the front door unassisted.

If someone else escorts your caller to the office, stand up, come from behind your desk and extend your hand. It is considerate and helpful to indicate where your guest should sit, particularly if there are choices.

When the appointment is over, either walk your caller to the outside door or to the elevator. You might ask your secretary to do it, but that extra bit of attention on your part will be well worth it in your business relations.

If your business caller seems to be staying overlong and you need to attend to other business, rise to indicate that your appointment is over. If your guest doesn't seem to get the hint, you can try moving toward the door. Hopefully that will do it. If you have a full schedule, it is perfectly acceptable to have your secretary or a co-worker come to your door and advise you politely of your next appointment.

Respecting Space in the Workplace

Have you ever returned to your office from a well-deserved vacation and had the distinct feeling that your office or desk had become public property during your absence? Perhaps the crumbs that you found next to your keyboard did not match those of the last lunch you ate at your desk before you left, and the Rolodex was flipped to the name of someone you had not called in years.

Good manners require that we respect the space and the privacy of others in the workplace, and that they do the same for us.

If you have a meeting in someone's office, don't go in until you have been invited to do so. Even if the door is open, knock and wait to be acknowledged before entering. If the person is on the phone, remain outside unless you receive a signal to enter.

If the person with whom you are meeting must take a phone call while you are there, ask if you should leave for a moment. Good manners dictate that the person with whom you are meeting would alert you to the possibility of an incoming call and would indicate whether you should step out or remain in the office.

Always ask permission before you place your coffee cup, files or papers on someone else's desk. After all, that is the other person's space.

Ask permission before you use a co-worker's desk, office equipment or supplies. If other people are away from their desks, this is not an open invitation to make yourself at home. When you use someone's desk, leave things just as you found them. Whatever you borrow should be returned promptly and in good condition. Whatever you use up should be replaced.

Everyone in an office is responsible for maintaining shared space such as kitchens, boardrooms and copy rooms. If you use the last bit of copy paper, refill the machine. When supplies are low, replenish them or notify the person who is responsible for doing so. If you enjoy the benefits of an office kitchen, clean up after yourself. Remember — your mother doesn't work there!

Cubicle Etiquette

Many businesses today find it more economical and efficient to provide cubicles as workspace for their employees rather than private offices. While the impact on the bottom line is obvious, cubicles offer significant challenges to the office worker. Cubicles afford no privacy and a multitude of distractions.

The same rules apply to cubicles as to offices with traditional walls and doors. The absence of a door is not tantamount to a welcome sign. Wait until you are invited into someone's office. If the other person appears to be busy or doesn't make eye contact with you, go away. Don't sit down unless you are asked. For some cubicle occupants, a chair is a non-issue. They simply don't have one.

When you approach someone else's cubicle, the first words out of your mouth should be, "Is this a convenient time to talk to you?" Keep in mind that a visitor is an interruption.

Follow these simple rules of courtesy with regard to your cubicle space.

◊ Be careful what you discuss either on the phone or in person. Confidential or personal matters should be handled in private areas where you cannot be over-heard.

◊ Be considerate of co-workers by keeping your voice low and certainly never use a speaker phone.

◊ Keep your space neat and free from clutter. While some people treat a cubicle like a dorm room with personal pictures and posters everywhere, a messy space reflects poorly on you as a professional.

◊ Never be so thoughtless as to eat popcorn or pizza or other equally noxious foods at your desk. Your co-workers won't appreciate having their work inter-rupted by the smell of your snack or the sound of your smack.

Pets in the Office

A number of businesses today are adopting an "open dog" policy which has come about as a result of our informal office practices. After all when employees wear jeans to the office, call the CEO and the Chairman of the Board by their first names, why not bring Spot to work? If dogs are well mannered, well groomed and flea-free, they can make a positive contribution to the workplace. They can serve as icebreakers, conversation pieces, and in some cases, security guards. Pet owners are happier workers when they don't have to feel bad about leaving doggie home alone with only a few rawhide chews and a pair of old slippers. Some employees go so far as to say that pets in the office help to relieve stress. It is hard to be tense when someone is licking your knee.

Keep in mind that your clients come to see you, not your pet.

Pets in the office should be limited to those that qualify as traditional house pets. If you happen to be the proud owner of boa constrictor, leave it at home. Few of your customers, clients, or coworkers will feel at ease with a reptile slithering around the office.

Cats should be left at home. Unless you own a fish market and the cat lives on the premises, don't take kitty to work. While cats are the number one choice for a pet today, they are not, as a rule, as responsive and obedient as dogs. It is risky to have a cat at work because of the chance that it could slip away from you and become lost. Besides, cats look so comfortable when they are sleeping that everyone in the office will want to take a nap, too.

Don't give your dog free run of the facilities until you know how clients feel about animals. Keep the dog in a confined space such as a small office with a doggie gate across the door. This will allow you to introduce the dog to your customers gradually. If the customer's reaction to your dog is positive, then the dog can join your meeting. If the customer seems less than enthusiastic, leave Spot behind bars.

Keep your dog off the office furniture. Your customers don't want to leave wearing a fur coat unless they wore one in.

Make sure your office dog is obedient and relates well to strangers. If pets are not friendly, do not bring them to work to harass your customers and co-workers. Most people like pets and will enjoy the company of a well-behaved dog.

Check your liability policy. In the event your dog and your customer make physical contact of the wrong kind, it would be bad enough to lose a customer, without gaining a lawsuit in the process.

If you decide to institute pet days at the office, verify that all who participate of the four-legged variety have had their vaccinations and inoculations.

Between Doors and Floors

People get stuck all the time moving between floors and doors. They get stuck wondering who goes first, who holds the door and what to do about slow moving traffic. Mostly, people are caught between the old and the new etiquette. It used to be quite simple — ladies first. In today's business world where manners are not gender-driven, the rule that prevails is one of common sense — when in doubt, do what is practical and courteous.

The rule of the door: Whoever gets there first opens it. No more hanging back waiting to see who will open it or hold it. By all means, if you get to the door first, look to see if you can hold it for someone else. It is rude to let a door shut in someone else's face. If you are escorting a client or a visitor, of course, you should position yourself to open and hold the door for your guest.

Always say "Thank you" to the person who holds the door.

The rule of the elevator: Make way for others. Never rush on to an elevator before others can exit. If you are waiting to get on an elevator, stand back from the door so that those people trying to exit may do so comfortably. The only reason for being in that great a hurry would be if the building were on fire. In that case, you shouldn't be using the elevator anyway.

Gender doesn't count on elevators. While it is considerate for a man to stand back and let a woman precede him through a doorway, this old rule of etiquette generates confusion and often results in traffic jams on elevators. When the elevator door opens, the person closest to the door should exit first. That person may opt to stand out of the way and hold the door for those who follow.

Always move as far back as you can on an elevator to allow room for others. However, if you are one of the first to enter the elevator and you will be getting off on the next floor, step to the side of the elevator rather than the back. It is a waste of everyone's time if ten people have to exit to let one off.

The rule of the stairs and escalator: Step aside, but no pushing.
The rules of the stairs are similar to the rules of the road. Slow traffic should stay to the right. This allows people who need to move faster to pass on the left on stairs and escalators.

Slow traffic should stay to the right on moving sidewalks.

The rule of the revolving door: One at a time and keep moving.
As with other doors, the person who arrives first goes ahead. The host leads the way, gently pushing and meeting the guest on the other side. Whatever you do, keep the pace. If you slow down or stop, it throws everyone's momentum off and you will have fewer friends when you get to the other side.

Disability Etiquette

The Americans with Disabilities Act requires that persons with disabilities be provided access to public buildings and that businesses make provisions to facilitate the employment of these persons. For many people who previously had little contact with the physically and mentally disabled, their presence in the workplace has raised questions of how to interact with them in ways that are courteous and respectful. Basic kindness and good common sense should guide your behavior in these situations as in all others.

When a person with a disability is accompanied by a companion, look at and speak directly to the person with the disability. Don't treat the companion as an interpreter or act as if people with disabilities cannot communicate for themselves.

Persons who are wheelchair-bound are not hearing-impaired. For some reason, we want to speak louder than normal to someone who is in a wheelchair as if that person had problems with hearing. Speak to those persons in normal tones.

Show respect by not leaning on a person's wheelchair.

Questions and comments about the impairment or disability are not appropriate. Unless the person with the disability brings up the subject of the condition, you should not. There are sufficient topics for conversation without being intrusive.

When you are speaking to someone who is hearing impaired, look right at the person and don't start speaking until you have that person's attention.

Offer assistance but wait for the disabled person to accept your help and explain how you can assist. Most disabled people are accustomed to doing things for themselves and acting independently. If your offer to help is accepted, wait to be told how you can assist. Don't assume that you know what is needed or how to do it.

If someone has a visual impairment and uses a seeing-eye dog for assistance, don't treat the dog as a pet. The dog is working for that person and should not be distracted.

Know the terminology for persons with disabilities. The focus is on the person rather than the disability. You would talk about a "person with epilepsy" rather than an "epileptic." It is important to choose your words thoughtfully and carefully. Remember that you want to be respectful and courteous.

Avoid such terms as:	*Instead say:*
Wheelchair bound	Person who uses a wheelchair
Blind	Visually-impaired
Deaf	Hearing-impaired
Cripple	Person with a disability

Handicapped is an outdated term. Today, a person with a handicap is a golfer.

Your Notes Here

Your Notes Here

Chapter Nine

GIFT-GIVING IN BUSINESS

Gift-giving is a way of developing and maintaining relationships in business. It may be done between the company and its customers, between the company and its employees or among employees within the company.

When handled in the right way, gifts bring pleasure to the giver and the recipient. Done improperly, gift giving can create problems and generate negative feelings. Before you venture forth to purchase that business gift, you need to consider a number of factors including but not limited to selection and presentation.

Considerations in Giving Gifts

< Company Policy >

Know the company policy. That means being aware of your company's policy and the policy of the recipient's company. It is easy enough to check within your own organization; however, it may not be so simple to find out if your customer may accept a gift. If you have any doubts, be prepared that your gift might be refused and accept the refusal graciously.

< Company Tradition >

Learn what the gift giving traditions are in your organization. Know who generally gives to whom within the organization and within departments. If you are new to the company, ask others how gifts are handled on special occasions. Depending on your position, you may decide to start a new tradition, but be sensitive to what has gone on before.

< Gift-Giving Occasions >

The occasion being celebrated or the event being recognized influence the type of gift you choose. The occasions for giving gifts in business fall into six categories: family, personal, company, employee recognition, thank you and holiday.

Family events are births, weddings, and funerals. These clearly fall outside the world of work, but are occasions that need to be recognized because of their significance to the employee.

Personal occasions are birthdays and illness. Often a card is the best way to acknowledge these events. Birthday celebrations and gifts can become major office happenings that some people look forward to and others learn to dread. Think of keeping recognition simple and appropriate. Just because the employee is your best friend doesn't mean that the rest of the department wants to spend a lot of time and money on the celebration. When there is an illness, flowers and plants are good choices and they are appreciated by practically everyone.

Company occasions include promotions, retirement and employee milestones. The organization usually has a standard gift and a procedure for recognizing these occurrences. Secretary's Day and Bosses' Day have become popular office traditions and fall into the category of employee recognition. Balloon and flower sales generally soar on these special days.

Sadly, thank-you gifts in the office are the exception rather than the rule. Bosses and managers tend to think that the paycheck is all the thanks that an employee needs. Gifts of appreciation can be simple, inexpensive, and still be very effective. A special parking space for a week, a small plant for the desk, or some extra time off with pay are easy to give and can go a long way in boosting morale and recognizing good work or extra effort.

Holiday gifts focus on the religious year-end holidays. Being sensitive to diversity in the workplace today is critical. The gifts you give should be in line with the holidays that your customers and co-workers observe.

The Relationship

In giving gifts in business, the relationship between the giver and the recipient makes a difference. It is not simply a matter of personal relationship, but of hierarchy, which determines whether the gesture is appropriate. Once again company policy should be considered.

Bosses may give gifts to their employees on whatever occasions they choose. This is based largely on a presumption of greater income and ability to give. However, bosses should make every effort to be fair-minded and evenhanded in giving gifts. Consideration should also be given to how other departments within an organization handle employee gifts.

Employees do not generally give their bosses gifts. An entire department may join together to purchase a birthday or holiday present if they wish, or a single employee may take a hostess gift to the holiday party at the boss's home. Any thing more lavish appears to curry favor or is simply in poor taste.

Gift giving between employees is a personal choice. Many offices like to celebrate birthdays and holidays by giving presents. Be aware that not everyone is enthusiastic about constantly having the hat passed for employee birthdays. If most people in the office want to celebrate, establish a clear policy about how much is collected per person and honor those who may not want to be involved.

The exchange of gifts between client, customer, vendor and the company representative should be approached with caution. These gifts may be given for all the right reasons, but we all know which road is paved with good intentions. Check company policy and consider the cost and appropriateness of the gift. Small gifts with the company logo will not raise questions, but more lavish gifts may be construed as an attempt to influence business and should not be accepted.

The Cost

Deciding how much to spend on a gift is a difficult issue. The lines between cheap and extravagant are often blurred. Four factors should guide you in deciding how much to spend: company policy, company tradition, your salary, and the number of people giving the gift.

The Gift

People probably agonize the most over what gift to give, particularly when they are making an effort to personalize the gift. If you are sending a gift of celebration, condolence or thanks, flowers or plants are easy and always appropriate. For holiday and hostess giving, foods and wine are good choices.

Determine whether you want the gift to be of a personal nature or if you want it to be for office use. If your gift is to be personal, you need to know something about the hobbies or interests of the recipient, being careful that your gift is not too personal. Items of clothing and fragrance would be considered inappropriate. Giving careful thought to the tastes and the preferences of the person to whom you are giving a gift will prevent it from ending up in the recycle bin.

A word about corporate gifts. The gifts you give to your customers and clients should reflect well on your company. When you put your logo on an item, be certain that it sends a strong positive message to all who will see it.

The Presentation

The presentation of your gift should be handled with as much thought and care as the selection of the gift. It makes no sense to spend hours choosing the perfect present and hard earned dollars purchasing it, and not wrap it attractively or present it personally. A festively wrapped package can bring as much pleasure as the gift itself. If you aren't good at wrapping, enlist someone who is. Your gift should be accompanied by a personally signed card.

The most effective way to present a gift is to do it in person.

Accepting Gifts

When accepting a gift, you want the giver to feel your pleasure by showing appreciation and enthusiasm. Even if you aren't particularly thrilled with the item, make other people believe that you are. Remember that you are showing appreciation for their thoughtfulness. Thank them graciously in person, and then send a written note within twenty-four to forty-eight hours.

Refusing Gifts

If you receive a gift that you cannot accept, return it within twenty-four hours with a note that explains why you have to refuse it. It is either against company policy for you to accept it or it is not appropriate. If the gift came with the wrong intentions, document having returned it.

Your Notes Here

Your Notes Here

Your Notes Here

Chapter Ten

ETIQUETTE OUT OF THE OFFICE

Travel has become a necessary part of business. The way you conduct yourself while traveling will reflect not only on you but also on your organization. The woman who lost her temper and kicked the seat of the passenger in front of her on an airplane was identified in the news by the company for whom she worked. Business travel has become stressful enough without having to bear the burden of being under scrutiny twenty-four hours a day. However, the reality is that you are.

Travel by Car

Not all business people are in the air these days, although it may seem like it to those who fly. Many people are traveling by car. Often they are traveling with others, either their bosses or their colleagues. While this is not a complicated subject, there are rules to follow when traveling by car whether it is by private car, taxi or limousine.

The person who owns the car drives. Offering to do some of the driving is a nice gesture when the car is not yours. Stating your offer twice lets the driver know that you are sincere, but don't insist beyond that.

If there are other passengers along, ask where you should sit. The choice seat is reserved for the senior person. If that doesn't happen to be you, wait for an indication of where you should ride, or simply ask.

The client always gets the preferred seat.

If you are driving, keep your emotions in check. Road rage, a legacy of the 1990s, is not becoming to anyone and certainly will do nothing to further your business relations. A valid driver's license does not give people permission to be rude.

When you are traveling by cab or limo, remember that the best seat is the on the passenger side in the rear. Observe the rank and hierarchy of the other passengers in determining who takes this seat. Gender doesn't count.

If you are with a group traveling by limo, the most uncomfortable seats go to the persons of lesser rank. Junior executives take the middle seats. If someone has to sit up front with the driver, the partition should be left open so that person does not feel isolated from the group. This applies to taxis and limos.

From curbside, the person of lower rank enters the cab or limo first and slides across to the undesirable seat.

Flying Etiquette

At a time when many business people are in the air as much as they are in their automobiles, the subject of airplane etiquette takes on new significance. As airlines find more ways to squeeze a greater number of passengers into less space, those who fly need to know and to observe the rules of manners in these tight spaces.

Observe the carryon limit of two bags. It is understandable that passengers want to avoid both the inconvenience of lost luggage and the delay in baggage pickup, but if your bags exceed the size and the number for carryon, don't try to beat the system. Chances are you will be detected at check-in. If you make it past that point and your bags won't fit in the overhead bin, you delay everyone else while your bags have to be removed. If you manage to slip by with an excess number and fit them all overhead, you are taking storage space from other passengers.

Be aware of others as you carry your bags onto the plane and down the aisle so that you don't bruise those passengers seated on the aisle with hits from your luggage. Even backpacks, diaper bags and handbags can do bodily harm. If you do land a blow, ask forgiveness.

Be polite to your seatmates, but respect their privacy. By all means acknowledge those next to you with a friendly greeting, but don't try to force conversation. Not everyone is an extrovert with a need to socialize. People who are traveling on business use their flying time to accomplish work or catch up on their sleep. A brief exchange of small talk will usually be enough to let you know if the person sitting next to you wants to engage in conversation, complete a business report or enjoy some well-deserved private time.

When you recline your seat, remember that the people behind you have legs. Few airlines allow for this. Recline your seat slowly and listen for any audible screams. If you are aware that someone behind you is trying to get out into the aisle, pull your seatback up. Most of us have a hard time doing the limbo at 30,000 feet.

When your flight is late arriving at its destination, be considerate of passengers with a short connecting time. If you don't have a connecting flight, heed the flight attendant's plea and remain seated until those who are hurrying to make their connections have exited. You will appreciate this act of courtesy the next time you have only minutes to travel between gates.

It is the responsibility of a junior executive when traveling with a senior executive to handle tipping, cab fare, checking in and out of hotels and paying for the restaurant tabs.

Hotel Accommodations

A word about hotel stays — do not conduct business in your hotel room. This is not the appropriate setting for a business meeting. While your intentions may be entirely above board, you can send the wrong message by using your room for business. Hotels have plenty of space for that purpose so avail yourself of a good meeting room.

Meeting Etiquette

Meetings are a major part of our business life. How often have you questioned the amount of time you spend in meetings? Management people spend anywhere from 35-60% of their workweek in meetings. Some of these are necessary, some are not, but all meetings are costly. While people are in meetings, work piles up, messages collect, and customers wait.

Pay attention to how you plan meetings and how you carry them out so that they are efficient and effective. Good manners in business dictate that you be considerate and courteous in using other people's time. Whether you are the leader or a participant, there are specific ways to insure that your meetings are productive and useful.

Well-run meetings result in improved business practices and better business relationships.

Planning and Preparation

Most of the bad press that meetings receive is the result of poor planning or no planning. Nobody should call a meeting without giving sufficient thought as to why the meeting is necessary, who should attend, where it should be held, what items need to be covered, what the order of business should be, what the rules of behavior are, and finally how participants will be notified.

The first step in planning is to decide if the meeting is necessary. There are people who meet for the sake of meeting. Business time is too precious to be wasted like that. Think about what you need to accomplish. Is it necessary to bring people together or can the same results be obtained through a phone call, a voice mail message, a memo or an e-mail message? If a meeting is necessary, is there information that can be sent out ahead of time to shorten the actual time spent in the meeting?

Many meetings can either be avoided altogether or shortened significantly. Both are good options.

Thoughtfully select participants. Another pitfall of meeting planners is not giving enough attention to who should attend. It is important to know who to invite and who not to invite. Only those people who have information to share, those who have to receive the information, or those who need to be involved in the decision or in its implementation ought to be included.

Not everybody and his brother should attend every meeting. The more the merrier is a poor theory to employ for planning.

The 3M Meeting Management Institute suggests that fewer than five people are best for decision-making. Between five and ten are effective for problem solving. Larger groups are effective when your intent is to disseminate information or inspire participants.

When you are asked to attend a meeting and the objective is not clear, ask what the purpose is and why you have been included.

Give careful thought to where the meeting will be held. The environment can contribute to the success or failure of your meeting, and yet it is often given little attention. Convenience of the location, comfort of the room with regard to seating and lighting, and the privacy factor should all be taken into account in the planning process. If the location is not central for most participants or cannot be conveniently accessed, attendance will be affected. Some meetings fail simply because people can't find parking.

The meeting room should be comfortable. Uncomfortable people do not make good decisions nor do they stay long. Pay attention to ventilation and lighting in the room. Seeing and breathing are important considerations. The room should be large enough to accommodate all participants without squeezing them in.

Consider the privacy factor. Constant interruptions or nearby distractions will interfere with the flow of your meeting.

Arrange the room with your purpose in mind. Don't leave seating to chance. The room should be arranged according to what you want to accomplish. If you want decisions to be made or problems to be solved, choose a seating arrangement where participants can see and talk to each other easily. If you want to promote interaction, use a round table or a U-shaped table. If the leader needs recognition, choose a rectangular configuration. If information is to be presented, a theater or classroom style is best.

Other considerations for setting up a meeting include the use of nametags or tent cards to promote interaction and teamwork, audiovisual needs if information is to be shared, and whether or not refreshments are to be served.

Plan the agenda and circulate it prior to the meeting. If you have trouble deciding what to put on the agenda, maybe you should cancel the meeting. An agenda will help you to focus and to stay on course. Every meeting should have a clear time limit. By assigning a time to each item you can stay on a pre-determined schedule. If an item starts to go over its designated time, participants can decide how to handle it with respect to the overall meeting time and other pieces of business.

Unless you are negotiating world peace or a national labor dispute, no meeting should go on endlessly. When meetings last more than 1 1/2 hours, participation starts to lag and interest wanes.

Your meeting will run more smoothly if you circulate the agenda in advance. Participants will feel better informed and will come ready to discuss issues. By all means, consult other participants for input on the agenda. If you assign agenda items to specific people, ask their permission in advance.

Establish clear ground rules for your meetings. By establishing rules of conduct, you will limit unproductive behavior. Ask the group to participate in creating the rules. Reiterate them from time to time. Groups that meet frequently like to post their ground rules each time. The most common ones that can apply to meetings are:

◊   Keep an open mind.
◊   Stay on the subject.
◊   Ask questions.
◊   Participate.
◊   Listen to what others are saying.
◊   Observe break times.
◊   Respect the confidentiality of the meeting.

Establish a system for evaluating your meetings. Too often this key aspect of planning is overlooked. Meeting evaluation can be as formal as a written questionnaire or it can be as informal as a few phone calls after the fact to select participants. This important feedback will help you plan future meetings.

Being an Effective Meeting Leader

An effective leader plans thoughtfully and carefully, then manages the flow of the meeting. This requires that the leader maintain control of time and people while skillfully involving all participants. The good leader is one who:

◊ Begins and ends the meeting on time.
◊ Introduces newcomers to the group.
◊ Keeps participants focused on the issues and on the agenda.
◊ Involves everyone in discussion.
◊ Does not let one or two persons dominate.
◊ Allows for questions and facilitates discussion.
◊ Is aware of feelings and nonverbal communication.
◊ Gives credit to everyone who helped or participated in the meeting.
◊ Sets a date and time for the next meeting.
◊ Makes certain that participants understand their responsibility for follow-up.

Being an Effective Participant

The responsibility for the success of the meeting lies with participants as well as the leader. The effective participant is one who:

◊ Prepares for the meeting by receiving and reading all material circulated.
◊ Arrives on time for the meeting.
◊ Contributes ideas to the discussion.
◊ Listens to other people's ideas.
◊ Approaches issues objectively.
◊ Does not rush to judgment.
◊ Stays focused and attentive.

◊   Takes notes.
◊   Provides feedback to the leader.
◊   Follows up on agreed action after the meeting.

Following the Meeting

When the meeting is over, both the leader and the participants should take responsibility for seeing that the space is left in order. The appropriate people need be thanked for assisting with the meeting. Evaluations should be completed, formally or informally. Minutes should be written and sent out within a few days while people can still remember and agree upon the content of the meeting.

Volunteer Etiquette

Business people provide much of the volunteer leadership and the unpaid workforce for the nonprofit sector. The reasons that people volunteer are as individual as the volunteers themselves. Some people volunteer unselfishly because they want to support a particular cause or to be of service to the community. Other people volunteer for personal gain like individual recognition, an opportunity to network with community leaders, a chance to gain skills or the need to build a resumé. Unless the reasons for volunteering are immoral or illegitimate, it does not matter to the agency why people give their time and energy. The ever-expanding nonprofit sector stands to win from the involvement of the business community. Those who give freely of their time and talent need to follow specific rules of behavior.

The act of volunteering does not give license to behave any way you choose.

Volunteers should be reliable. Agencies depend on volunteers to come when they promise. Work doesn't get done when volunteers fail to show. If the task is important enough to assign to a volunteer, it needs to be done.

If you must be absent from your volunteer assignment, let someone know and give enough notice so that your position can be covered. Find out whom you should notify in case of absence.

Follow through on your commitments. If you promise to complete a task or take responsibility for an activity or event, see it through. If you realize that you cannot do a job, let the agency know. Volunteers have been known to ride off into the sunset without a word rather than confess that they can't complete a task. This is extremely unfair to those who are counting on you.

Don't agree to take a job that you know you cannot do. If a task is too time-consuming for your schedule, admit it and negotiate for a part of the job that you can manage. The beauty of volunteering is that you can select the parts of the assignment that match your time and talents.

Learn how to say "no." Volunteers are by nature helpful people who have a hard time walking away from a job that needs to be done. Be realistic in what you can do so that you don't burn out and let the agency down.

Treat the staff as the experts that they are. Volunteers often see things from a different perspective from paid staff who work in the area every day. While your advice and assistance are helpful, respect the experience of the staff.

Be knowledgeable about the organization. Take advantage of every opportunity to learn all that you can about the people, the cause and the system. The more you know about the organization, the more valuable you will be as a volunteer. Attend all required meetings and training sessions and read all the information that is sent to you.

Treat all information that you learn while volunteering as confidential. You will be trusted with information about people and programs that is not to be passed on outside the agency. Any breach of confidentiality is grounds for separation from an organization.

Be a community spokesperson for the organization. One of the major benefits of having volunteers is that they increase the visibility of an organization. Be an active and positive supporter by carrying the message about the agency and its mission to the community. If you cannot be an outspoken advocate, consider another agency.

Don't be a complainer and a whiner. People get paid to do that so you don't have to.

Do not expect or accept compensation for your volunteer work. An increasing number of volunteers are receiving compensation for their work in the form of stipends and tangible benefits. It is one thing to be reimbursed for some of the costs of volunteering such as transportation and uniforms; but if you go into it expecting paid benefits, it may no longer be volunteering. Don't lose sight of the fact that volunteering is an unselfish act of giving, not of receiving. Volunteer benefits are a bonus.

As a business person volunteering in the community, your actions will reflect on your company as well as you personally.

Your Notes Here

Your Notes Here

Your Notes Here

Chapter Eleven

DINING FOR PROFIT

So much business is conducted over meals today that the successful professional dares not venture out without knowing good table manners. Whether the purpose of the meal is to win over a customer, enhance a client relationship, impress a potential employer or acquire a promotion, you want to feel confident and at ease in any dining situation. This involves knowing which meal is appropriate for the business you need to conduct, understanding your role as either host or guest and being competent with the foods and utensils that are presented. You can't concentrate on the business at a hand if you are worried about which fork to use, how to eat the pasta or what to do with the olive pit in your mouth.

Breakfast, Lunch, or Dinner

While the most popular business meal is lunch, there are times when you might want to meet for breakfast or dinner. Most of us have such busy schedules that it is often difficult to find time during the day to meet. Breakfast meetings are a good choice when you want to save time and avoid interruptions during the workday. They are usually less formal and less expensive. They are brief because most people are concerned about getting to the office to start the day.

The business dinner is more formal than other meals, with additional utensils and courses to manage. It is more expensive than breakfast or lunch and tends to be a more social occasion. Because the business dinner offers the opportunity to include spouses or other guests, conversation related to business may be limited. This is not the time to get into "hard-core" issues. Another consideration at dinner is that wine and alcoholic beverages are usually served. At business functions you may want to watch the alcohol you drink so you don't embarrass yourself or give away the corporate secrets.

Lunch remains the business meal of choice since it comes in the middle of the workday and doesn't infringe on personal time. For people who are concerned with keeping the balance between personal and professional life, this is a significant consideration. Lunch is a less costly meal, and alcohol can be avoided. Lunch will not be as brief as breakfast, but it does have time limitations since people need to return to work.

Afternoon Tea

The recent popularity of afternoon tea gives business people another option for business dining. Afternoon tea is served between 2:30 and 5:00 PM, depending on the location. It is a nice alternative to other business meals because it does not have to be an interruption of the workday, and it doesn't infringe on personal time. You can meet someone for afternoon tea, spend 45 minutes to an hour and head for home aferwards. Because of the benefits of tea, you may even find that you are brighter and more energetic after a tea break. In that case, you may want to meet for tea and then return to the office.

The term "high tea" is often confused with afternoon tea. In distinguishing between the two, afternoon tea is served with finger sandwiches, scones and sweets. High tea, served after 5 o'clock, is a much heartier meal which originated with the working class, looking for a substantial meal at the end of a day of labor in the fields and factories.

Hosting the Business Meal

The business meal requires the same attention to detail as any other business activity or event. When you are the host, you need to manage each step of the process from choosing the restaurant to planning the seating and handling the bill.

As the host, it is your responsibility to select the restaurant. Your choice of a restaurant will contribute to the success or failure of your meeting. Choose a restaurant with which you are familiar so that you know the food, the atmosphere and the staff. This is not the time to try out the new place in town. You should know that the food is good and will offer appropriate choices for your guest, that the atmosphere is conducive to discussing business and that the staff will be responsive to your needs. The restaurant that you select should be convenient for your guest.

If you are entertaining away from home, ask the hotel concierge or someone you know — and whose taste you trust — to recommend a restaurant. In this case, it is acceptable to ask your guest for suggestions or favorite restaurants to guide you. However, you put your guest in an awkward situation when that person is not sure of your price range or your expectations.

Reconfirm on the day of the meal. Make two phone calls: one to the restaurant to verify your reservations and the other to your guest to confirm the arrangements. Be very clear about when and where you will meet.

Arrive ahead of your guest. Be sure that you are not only on time, but also that you arrive early. Your guest should not be kept waiting. It is uncomfortable and embarrassing for a guest to wait alone in what may be unfamiliar territory. If you see that you will be late, call and ask to have your guest seated.

If you are the first one to arrive at the table, do not order a drink, put your napkin in your lap, eat a roll, or disturb the place setting in any way. The table should be pristine clean when others arrive.

Make it clear in advance that you will be paying the bill. There is nothing that ruins the mood more than grappling over the check at the end of the meal. When you issue the invitation, state clearly that you would like for the other person to be your guest. If possible, make arrangements ahead of time to take care of the bill. If not, quietly let the waiter know at the beginning of the meal to bring you the bill. If your plans to handle the bill surreptitiously fail, be prepared to pick up the check as soon as the waiter brings it to the table. Don't let your guest wonder for even a second what your intentions are.

Allow yourself plenty of time for the meal. You don't want to make your guest feel rushed or have to excuse yourself to leave early. If you have an unavoidable engagement and are concerned about the time, make this known either when you issue the invitation or at the start of the meal.

Give your guest the best seat at the table. The seat with the view, or the one which looks out into the restaurant, should be given to your guest. No guest should have to stare at a blank wall, face the kitchen or watch the restroom traffic.

Allow your guests to order first but offer suggestions to guide them. By mentioning how much you enjoy certain items, you are conveying a price range. If you suggest appetizers that you like, you are encouraging your guest to order one. If you hadn't planned to order an appetizer and your guest does, have one yourself so the guest will not be embarrassed.

The primary duty of the host is to make the guest feel at ease.

Seating Your Guests

The host is responsible for handling the seating arrangements, taking care to give the guests the preferred seats. Seating becomes more complicated depending on the number of people and whether or not spouses are included.

If you have only one guest, seat that person next to you rather than across the table. If you have two guests, put one across the table from you and the other to the side. If you have them on either side of you, you will think you've spent a day at Wimbledon before the meal is over.

If you are hosting several guests, the most important one is seated to your right; the second most important is seated to your left. When there is a co-host, the co-host is seated at the opposite end of the table and the third most important guest would be on the co-host's right. Follow this protocol regardless of gender for business meals.

The place of honor is to the right of the host.

When spouses are included, the spouse of the guest is treated as if that person held the same rank as the husband or wife. The number one male guest and his spouse are treated the same. For example, if the host is a man, the spouse of the number one male guest is placed to the host's right. The number one guest is seated to the right of the host's wife. In the event that the spouse holds rank, the spouse is seated according to the rank held. This is clearly an issue that should not be left until the last minute for consideration. A wrong move and your business relationship could suffer.

The Role of the Guest

The guest has fewer responsibilities than the host, but they are equally significant. Always be on time. If you arrive more than five minutes early, walk around the block or otherwise occupy yourself. If you arrive before your host, the wait staff may be instructed to seat you. If that is the case, do not take your napkin off the table, order a drink or eat the bread while you wait. The table should be undisturbed when the host appears. Following the meal, send that written thank-you note within twenty-four hours.

If there are any problems with your food, let your host handle it with the staff.

When to Start Eating

The signal to begin eating is when the host or hostess has lifted the appropriate utensil. If there is not a specific host at your table, wait until everyone has been served before you begin. At large tables which seat eight or ten, the wait staff may have difficulty serving everyone at the same time. It is considerate of those who are waiting for their food to encourage others to start while their food is warm. If you are seated at a round table of six to ten, wait until all have been served before you begin eating. If you are seated at a long banquet table, begin eating when at least three people on either side of you have been served.

Managing The Napkin

There are signals for removing the napkin from the table. One is after the host does so. If there is no host at the table, wait until everyone at the table has been seated. In fine restaurants, the server will usually take the napkin from the table and place it in your lap for you.

When you remove your napkin, open it gently over your lap. A large dinner napkin is placed in your lap, folded in half with the crease closest to your waist. A luncheon napkin, which is smaller, is opened all the way. Never tuck the napkin into your clothing, either at the waist or the chin. If you are worried about your clothes, either learn to eat more carefully or buy washable fabrics.

Men's ties should never be tossed back across the shoulder to get them out of harm's way. Remember that the tie was actually designed to protect the shirt.

The napkin is used for blotting your mouth, not serious wiping. Of course, it is never used for mopping your brow at the table.

If you are concerned about your lipstick coming off on your napkin, blot it with a tissue before you come to the table. Lipstick on napkins or glasses is most unattractive and is harmful to a woman's professional image.

If you need to excuse yourself from the table during a meal, do so between courses. Place your napkin in your chair. Never put your napkin back on the table until everyone has finished.

When the meal is over, the host will place the napkin on the table. If there is no host, wait until everyone has finished and then put your napkin to the right of your place setting. The most appropriate time to do this is as everyone is rising from the table.

The Place Setting

The place setting serves much like the road map for your meal. When you sit down for a meal, you only have to look at the way the table is set to figure out what courses you will be eating and which beverages will be offered. The utensils that you will be using should be on the table. In the case of a very formal dinner, some of the flatware may be added or replaced with each course.

Forks are placed on the left with the napkin, and the knives and spoons are on the right with the glasses. Utensils are used from the outside in. For example, if there are two forks on the left, you will use the one on the outside first. At a formal dinner the fish course is served before the meat course so the fish fork is placed to the outside of the dinner fork. If you are going to be served soup as the first course, a soup spoon will be placed on the outside right of the place setting.

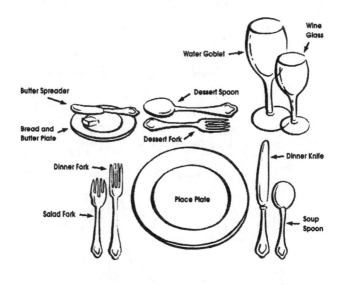

A Simple Place Setting

Liquids are placed on the right; solids on the left.

Your glassware will be to the right of the place setting. When you are seated, you will see all the glasses at once and know immediately how many different beverages will be served. At a formal dinner there will be numerous glasses, indicating that you will have several wines plus water. You will have a glass each for red and white wine, possibly a glass for sherry and one for champagne. At a less formal dinner, there may only be one wineglass as it will be an "either/or" situation — either red wine or white wine.

The red wine glass is held by the bowl, and the white wine glass is held by the stem to avoid warming the wine.

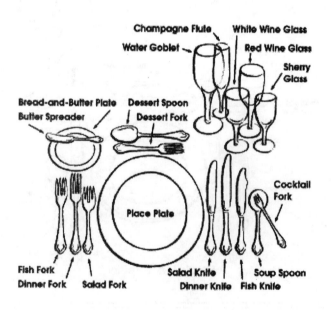

A Formal Place Setting

Bread and butter plates and salad plates are placed to the left. Many a poor soul at a seated luncheon or dinner has confused an entire table by choosing the wrong bread and butter plate. If the person on your left decides to lay claim to your bread plate, let it go. Place your bread on a plate which you are currently using. If you are between courses and don't have a plate, wait until one comes along before taking the bread. It is not worth creating an embarrassing situation for anyone.

The dessert fork and spoon are placed at the top of the place setting. They are set there before the meal unless it is a very formal meal. In that instance, they are brought to the table with the finger bowl.

American and Continental Styles of Eating

There are two styles of eating in this country: American and Continental. Since both are acceptable, the choice is yours. Many business people are adopting the Continental style because it appears to be more efficient and more graceful than the zigzag American style. Whichever one you select, be consistent and be correct. It is not acceptable to switch back and forth from one style to the other as it suits you during the course. For instance, if you begin eating the entree using the Continental style, which works so well when cutting and eating the meat, then run into trouble with the green peas, switching to American style at this point is not cricket. My

Cutting Food
American &
Continental Style

advice to all who are intrigued with the Continental way of eating is to observe those who use it correctly. Practice in private or with family and friends so that you know what you are doing when you take your show on the road.

For the American style, these are the steps to follow:

1. Cut your food with your fork in your left hand and the knife in the right.

Cut only one piece of food at a time. The reason that your mother used to cut all of your meat at once was so that she could eat her dinner uninterrupted, not because it was the correct way to eat.

---

2. To take the food to your mouth, place the knife with the blade facing in or toward you at the top of the plate. Then transfer the fork to your right hand and place the food in your mouth with the tines of the fork up.

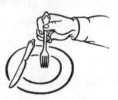

Bringing Food to Your Mouth American Style

3. Between bites leave the knife at the top of the plate

Resting Position American Style

and put your fork on the right side of the plate with the handle on the lower right side. It helps to picture the plate as a clock. In this case, the handle of the fork is resting over the imaginary four and the tines are pointing to the imaginary ten. Your fork, therefore, is in the 10:20 position. It doesn't matter if it is am or pm.

4. When you have finished eating, place the fork in the 10:20 position and bring the knife down beside it.

Finished Position American Style (Tines Up)

> **When you have finished eating, please don't say that you are done. People are "finished." Cakes are "done."**

For eating Continental style, follow these steps:

1   Keep the fork in your right hand and the knife in your left hand throughout the meal unless you are resting. Cut the food as you would in the American style. With

the tines down, you may use the knife to push food onto the back of the fork. When you are ready to put the food in your mouth, do so with the tines still down. Otherwise everything you so carefully pushed onto the back of the fork will fall off and you will have to start over.

Bringing Food to
Your Mouth
Continental Style

2   When you are resting between bites, place the knife first with the handle on the lower right side of your plate. The handle is resting over the imaginary four of the clock. Next place the fork on the left side of your plate with the handle resting over the imaginary eight on the clock, tines down. This forms something of an inverted V.

Resting Position
Continental Style
(Tines Down)

3   When you have finished, place the knife in the rest position — handle at four o'clock — and bring the fork over to the right side next to and below the knife, tines down. In keeping with the clock theme, this puts knife and fork at 10:20.

Finished Position
Continental Style
(Tines Down)

Eating Soup

Eating soup is not difficult but it does have its protocol. The issue is mainly the spoon, how to use it and where to place it. When eating soup, the spoon is taken away from you to the outside of the bowl or plate. Should a drop fall, it will land in the bowl and not on you. Clear soups are eaten from the side of the spoon and soups with "objects" in them like meat and vegetables are eaten from the front of the spoon. There are differing opinions about whether and when you may drink soup from the bowl. If the bowl has handles, you may lift the bowl to drink a clear broth. You may tip the bowl away from you to get the last drop. My best advice on lifting the bowl to drink from it is to let it go. The person with whom you are dining may not have read this chapter and will think that you are absolutely barbaric.

Place the soupspoon in the plate or bowl between spoonfuls. When you have finished, put the spoon on the saucer beside the bowl on the lower right hand side. If the soup is served in a shallow soup plate or dish, leave the spoon in the soup plate when you have finished. The handle should go on the right for easy removal by the wait staff.

If your soup is served in a narrow soup cup, place the spoon on the saucer between spoonfuls to avoid having your spoon standing straight up in the cup.

Buttering Your Bread

Bread should be eaten in bite-size pieces. First place the bread or roll on your bread and butter plate on the upper left side of the place setting. If you don't have a bread plate, put the bread on your entree plate. Next, tear off a bite-size piece, butter it and eat it. Repeat the procedure for each bite that you take. Never break the bread in half, cover it with butter and proceed to munch, and never cut your bread.

Be careful to put only small portions of food in your mouth at one time. What is more awkward than having someone ask you a question just as you start to chew?

Passing Foods

Foods are customarily passed to the right. Even if you are not having any, pass the rolls, butter and condiments to others. The cream and sugar should be placed on the table together within easy reach of the person next to you. When you pass the salt and pepper, keep them together. Items with handles, such as gravy boats, should be passed with the handle toward the other person.

Be thoughtful of those people who think it is bad luck to hand someone the salt. Always set the salt down in front of, or next to the person to whom you are passing it.

Ordering Wine

Ordering wine with your business meal can be an unsettling event when you are not confident about the process. Even if you are not a connoisseur of wine, you should know how to order it. Like all rules of etiquette, those dealing with the wine are pretty straightforward. The wine purist who pays more attention to the wine than his guests has no real place at today's business dinner.

You want to appear competent in ordering the wine without being a show-off.

If you don't know which wine to order, it is perfectly acceptable to ask the waiter or the sommelier (wine steward) for suggestions. The bottle will be brought to the table, unopened, for you to inspect and verify that it is what you ordered. Next the waiter will uncork the bottle and hand you the cork. You should feel it to determine if it is moist. If the cork is dry, the wine may not have been stored properly.

After you give your approval of the cork, the waiter will pour a small amount in your glass so that you can taste the wine. You are trying to determine if the wine is spoiled, not whether you like it. Occasionally wine has to be sent back. When you approve the selection, the wine is poured for your guests. The host is served last.

The wait staff will refill everyone's wine glass as needed. However the host should be attentive and refill the guest's glass if the waiter does not appear.

If you are the guest and prefer not to drink the wine, politely refuse. Never put your hand over the glass to indicate that you don't care to have any. If your glass is filled when you are not looking, you are not obligated to consume it. You can be sure that your glass will not be refilled if you do not drink any of the wine.

The old rule was to drink white wine with chicken or fish and red wine with red meats. Today, most people follow their personal preference. The key at the business dinner is to be more attentive to the amount of wine you drink rather than its color.

Words of Caution

Be careful about ordering food that you have never tried. If you have never tackled an artichoke before, don't try it when you are out with the boss discussing your promotion. Stay away from messy foods like onion soup and pasta. When the cheese in your soup turns to chewing gum and the strands of pasta become uncooperative, you will feel very uncomfortable. Whole lobster should be avoided, not only because it is a challenge to eat, but also because it is expensive.

Pace your eating so that you aren't the first or the last one to finish. If you have eaten almost everything on your plate and others are barely half way through, slow down. On the other hand if you see that you are well behind the others, eat a little faster or decide that you are not going to clean your plate. If you are involved in an interview or trying to close an important deal, you may have to do more talking and less eating. Don't make others wait for you to finish. Remember that there is always fast food on the way home.

Leave a little food on your plate to signify that you are satisfied. Members of the Clean Plate Club may give their host the idea that they did not have enough to eat.

If you have allergies or food restrictions, it is acceptable to ask how the food is prepared and to make a special request *in advance*. Don't make a big issue of your special needs.

If you are attending a large function where the meal is pre-ordered, tell the person issuing the invitation that you have special needs and inquire about the menu. It will cause confusion and give a poor impression if you wait to see what is served before you mention your dietary restrictions. If you haven't taken care of your special requests before hand, eat what you can on the plate and leave the rest.

Business meals are about business and are not the time to share foods or eat off someone else's plate.

Definitely a business meal is not the time to ask for a doggy bag. While half the population seems to think that all unconsumed food must be taken home for later consumption, and not usually by the dog, you will make a lasting impression of the wrong sort if you ask for the leftovers.

Hands belong on the table at a business meal, but arms and elbows do not. Rest your hands on the table at wrist level or slightly above. However, take care to maintain good posture, which does not allow for slumping over the table.

Mixing and Mingling at Business Receptions

Business receptions and cocktail parties provide excellent opportunities for networking and meeting with business colleagues in a social setting. These functions are a blend of business and pleasure. The key to making them successful for you and for your business is to maintain the balance between personal and professional.

Reply to the invitation promptly and correctly. Too many people have become lax about replying to invitations. They don't seem to realize that failure to reply is a lack of consideration for the host who needs to know the number of people who will be attending. The business invitation may include a reply card which makes it easy to respond and assures that the host will hear from most guests. Some invitations request a telephone reply and give a phone number and the name of the person who will be accepting responses.

RSVP is French for "répondez s'il vous plait" and is your signal that someone needs to hear from you. The best time for replying is as soon as you receive the invitation. Most people can look at a calendar and know immediately if the date is free. Why delay?

Make the most of the event by planning ahead. Know who will be there and why. Trouble yourself to find out something about the people that you will need to meet. Find out specific things about their background, hobbies or interests so that you can make conversation easily. If you can't find out anything about the people who will be at the function, think of several interesting topics that you might bring up in conversation.

Don't wait until you are standing face to face with a total stranger at a party to try to come up with something to discuss. The mind doesn't work that fast under stress.

When you arrive at a function, mix and mingle awhile before heading for the refreshments. Don't go straight for the bar or the hors d'oeuvres. You don't want to give the impression that you came for the food. If you know that you will be hungry and thirsty, eat or drink something before you go. When you do eat, don't hover over the food. Once again, these functions should be about business, not about food.

Introduce yourself to the people you don't know. Although it is not easy to approach strangers, remember that you are there to meet people. It is best to walk up to groups of three or more to introduce yourself. You are less likely to interrupt a private conversation if you approach several people at a time.

Work the crowd. Keep moving around so that you meet as many people as possible. If you know in advance whom you need to meet, your job will be easier. Smart business people don't stay in one place too long. They move around. If you find yourself stuck with one person, there are a number of ways to free yourself. Wait until you have finished speaking before you excuse yourself. If you excuse yourself as soon as others stop talking, they may wonder what they said wrong.

Don't clump with the people from your office or your nearest and dearest friends. The purpose of these events is to develop relationships and friendships with other businesspersons, and you can only do that by circulating. Take a moment to talk to friends or colleagues, but then get back to the business of mixing and mingling.

Keep your right hand free for handshaking. If you are not in the habit of carrying your beverage in your left hand, start now. You don't want to fumble around switching your glass from hand to hand, or extend a cold wet hand to the other person.

If nametags are provided, wear yours on your right shoulder so that it can be easily read when shaking hands.

Don't try to juggle a plate of food and a beverage unless you spent a summer working for Barnum and Bailey. While there is a technique for holding both a plate and a glass in one hand, I do not recommend it. It is simply not worth the risk if disaster strikes.

Know when to arrive and when to go home. Try to arrive at the beginning of the function. You will have a better chance of speaking to the people whom you need to contact. By all means leave before people start to wonder if you are part of the clean-up crew. It is always best to make your exit while others are still enjoying your company. If you tend to be one who stays overlong, decide in advance when you will leave and stick to it, no matter how much fun you are having.

Your Notes Here

Your Notes Here

Chapter Twelve

DOING BUSINESS INTERNATIONALLY

If you are not currently doing business internationally, chances are that you will be soon. When you interact with people from around the globe, whether they are your customers or your counterparts, you should be knowledgeable about their customs and sensitive to their culture.

No matter how skilled you are in your own industry, your expertise will not be enough if you are unaware of the business practices and social customs of your international partners. One small misstep such as using first names inappropriately, not observing the rules of timing or sending the wrong color flower to your hostess, can cost you the business relationship.

No one book and certainly no single chapter of a book can give you all the information that you need. Before you set out to do business internationally, read the books that deal specifically with that country. There are books that focus on Europe, books that focus on Asia, and books that focus on Latin America. Some books compile information on countries on several continents, and others deal in depth with the practices of a single country. Just be sure that when you embark on that international business trip, you have done all your homework. Your global counterparts will most assuredly have done theirs.

Don't make the mistake of thinking that you can learn all you need to know about another culture while you are visiting the country. In today's fast-paced business world, you may be on your way home before your ignorance has registered.

There are eight key areas in which you need to prepare yourself before you leave home:

1. Greetings and Introductions
2. Business Attire
3. Business Entertaining
4. Gift-giving
5. Appropriate Conversation
6. Gestures and Public Manners
7. Meeting Protocol
8. Punctuality

While the literature speaks in generalities about people from different cultures, keep in mind that you are dealing with individuals who are as different from one another as we North Americans are different from each other.

Greetings and Introductions

There are nearly as many ways to meet and greet people around the world as there are countries to visit. Since the way you handle your first encounter with your international partner will leave a lasting impression, be prepared to do it with confidence and ease. While the handshake is the most common form of greeting, the American style handshake with a firm grip, two quick pumps, eye contact and a smile is not universal. In some countries don't be surprised if you are greeted with a kiss, a hug, or a bow.

< Shaking Hands >

It would be wrong to make assumptions about other people based on the way they shake hands. The variations in handshakes are based on cultural differences, not on personality or values. The best rule to follow in shaking hands is to take your cue from your international hosts and follow their lead. If you are doing business in Japan, you will get a light handshake because that is the custom. In Germany, it will be firm with one pump, and in France it will be a light grip with a quick pump. In the Middle East expect continued shaking throughout the greeting.

Always extend the right hand to shake hands, which, of course, is customary in the United States. In parts of Africa, Asia and the Middle East there are taboos against using the left hand for anything. This applies to eating and gesturing as well as touching other people.

Knowing when, how often, and with whom to shake hands is another important factor in greetings. In most European countries, including Eastern Europe, you shake hands when you arrive and when you leave. It is often customary to begin with the most senior ranking person, not necessarily the person standing closest to you. Let the highest-ranking person, or the oldest person, initiate the handshake.

Handshaking between men and women around the globe is a complicated subject and one that should be carefully researched for each country. In the United States men and women routinely exchange handshakes in business, and it is no longer necessary to wait for the woman to extend her hand. Not so around the world.

When traveling around the world, learn when to initiate the handshake, and when to wait on others.

In most European countries, a business man waits for a woman to put out her hand. The woman should extend her hand in order not to lose credibility. While men and women are becoming more comfortable about shaking hands, we are not all there yet. In the Middle East men do not shake hands with women, and this is not an issue to force. In Asian countries, expect the same variations and do your homework country by country. In traveling from one Asian country to another as from one European country to another, don't assume that customs are the same. In some Asian countries women will shake hands, and in others, they offer the traditional bow.

< Hugging & Kissing >
Other forms of greeting include hugging and kissing. It is difficult for many Americans to react appropriately. Once again it pays to be prepared and know when to expect to be greeted in this fashion. In some European countries, you may encounter kissing on alternate cheeks, but this usually does not occur until the relationship has become more personal. The French are well known for this form of greeting. In Latin American countries, men engage in the "abrazo," a full embrace with several pats on the back. Know what is customary so you can react appropriately.

< Bowing >
Know how to bow. While most Asians have adopted the handshake as a form of respect in dealing with Westerners, you want to show the same consideration by learning how

and when to bow. This is particularly important when you do business in Japan. It is a seemingly small gesture, but a significant one. When you are bowing to someone on your same status level, bow at the same height. If you are bowing to someone of higher rank, bow slightly lower. If you are in doubt about the person's rank, err on the side of bowing lower.

Men bow with their hands at their sides, palms in. Women bow with their hands folded in front of them.

< Forms of Address >

Another aspect of greeting people involves using the proper form of address. We have become very informal in the United States and are quick to call people by their first names. Approach first names with caution around the world. Use titles and last names until you have been invited to use someone's first name. In some cases, as with your German and Dutch business partners, this may never occur. In most countries around the world, the use of first names is reserved for family and close friends. Thailand is quite an exception. People there are addressed by their title and first name, such as Mr. Bob and Ms. Linda. The reason for this is that last names were not used at all until the 20th century.

Titles are given more significance around the world than in the United States and are another important aspect of addressing business partners. Earned academic degrees are acknowledged. For example, in Germany an engineer is addressed as "Herr Ingenieur" and a professor as "Herr Professor." This is all the more reason to listen carefully when you are introduced to someone or to read a business card when you receive it.

**Knowing and using a person's correct title
signals respect.**

< Business Cards >

The exchange of business cards usually takes place during your initial business meeting. In some countries this exchange carries more significance than in others. Each country has its protocol when dealing with business cards. It is not simply a matter of when and how — it may also be a matter of what kind. While English is spoken around the world, it is presumptuous to expect that everyone you meet knows your language. In the Middle East and Asia, it is necessary to have bilingual business cards with English on one side and the language of the host country printed on the other side.

Know when to hand out business cards. In Japan where much attention is paid to ritual, wait until you have been introduced to give someone your card. However, as the visitor, you are expected to offer your card first. In Denmark, be ready to hand out your business cards at the beginning of a meeting, but in Italy, wait until after the initial meeting is over.

Know how to hand out your business cards. The key to giving out business cards in any culture is to show respect for the other person. Present your card with the native language side up so that the other person does not have to turn it over to read your information. In the Middle East, Africa, and Southeast Asia, remember to use your right hand. In Japan, China, Singapore, and Hong Kong, use both hands to present your card.

When you receive someone else's business card, always look at it and acknowledge it. When you put it away, place it carefully in your card case or with your business documents. Sticking it haphazardly in your pocket is demeaning to the giver. The Japanese place business cards on the table during the meeting.

Business cards — don't leave home without them. And if you are traveling in Asia, be sure to have plenty of them.

Business Attire

Dressing for business when you are traveling abroad is as confusing and varied as dressing for work in the United States. It all depends on where you are and with whom who you are doing business. While there are more similarities in business attire among European countries and while most Asians seem to follow the same dress rules, take nothing for granted.

Europeans as a rule dress more conservatively than we North Americans. The best guide for men to follow is to wear dark suits, starched shirts and ties. Women should dress in suits and business dresses with modest but quality jewelry. In France where fashion trends originate, quality and design are important. The Finns dress fashionably, but their neighbors in Norway prefer modest and practical attire. Eastern Europeans are not overly concerned with their appearance.

In most European and Asian countries, women do not wear slacks, even executive pants suits, in the workplace.

In Asia, business attire is conservative and the American business suit is the norm. When traveling in Asian countries, leave your business casual behind. For women, skirted suits and dresses are appropriate. Rarely is it acceptable for women to wear slacks in business or hemlines that are above the knee.

When doing business in countries where the climate is hot, pay attention to the fabrics that you wear. Rather than dressing down as we tend to do when the temperature rises, people in Asia and in Latin American make better choices about the fabrics they select.

Business Entertaining and Dining

Whenever you do business in another country, you can expect a certain amount of entertaining which, for the most part will center on dining. Each area has it unique foods and dishes and its own set of rules for how food is eaten. Know what to expect. Prepare yourself for your food adventures so that you can manage them with charm and grace.

In some countries, food is the focus and in others it is merely fuel for the body.

You may need to adjust your body clock to differences in meal times. In Latin America and in countries such as Israel and Italy, lunch may be the main meal of the day. Most people around the world eat both lunch and dinner later than we do. In Spain you can expect to have dinner between 9:30 and 11:00 P.M., and in Egypt, you'll have to wait until 10:30 at night to eat. Try to find out ahead of time when meals are taken and what is served so that you can avoid embarrassing and uncomfortable situations.

Find out which meals are appropriate for doing business. Americans do business over all meals, but this is not the case around the world. Breakfast meetings, which are quite popular and efficient in the United States, are not common worldwide. Breakfast meetings are often viewed as an intrusion on personal time. Although your host will invite you to dinner, do not expect to talk much business. Dinner is generally more of a social occasion. Japan is the exception. The Japanese like to wine and dine their guests, so expect to spend a long night with the Japanese and be prepared to do business.

When you travel, let your host be your guide in planning meetings over meals.

Find out when business is discussed at meals. In some countries, people want to get right down to business. The Germans are not fond of wasting time over small talk. However, in Spain, business won't be discussed until the end of the meal just when you had given up all hope.

No matter how anxious you are to talk business, let your foreign host begin the discussion.

How to eat food around the world is probably the most complex of all subjects. Some people eat with knives and forks, some with chopsticks and others with their fingers. Some people consider it rude to make noises when they eat and others are offended if their guests don't burp and slurp to indicate their enjoyment. "Boiling" international dining down to a few simple rules is all but impossible. If there are any universal guidelines, they are:

◊ Don't start eating before your host does. Waiting until the host begins is not only good manners but it also allows you to observe how foods are eaten. I have a friend who was dining with royalty in an Eastern country. A gorgeous salad was placed in front of her, but she wasn't quite sure when or how it was to be eaten. Being the savvy traveler and diplomat that she is, she waited for her host to eat the salad. It never happened and before she knew it, her beautiful salad was whisked away.

It is always a good idea no matter what country you are in to eat something before you go to a business meal. That way you won't be famished and go out of control when your food is served.

◊ Keep your hands above board. Unlike what your mothers and grandmothers always told you, your hands should be in view when you are eating around the world. This serves as a sign of openness. In cultures where food is eaten with the hands, putting them in your lap signals that you are finished.

◊ Eat a little bit of everything. To ignore or refuse certain items may be insulting to the host. You may not be thrilled that you have been served the equivalent of earthworms. If it is the local delicacy, your host probably went to some trouble to offer it to you, and you need to show appreciation. I always figure that if other people have been eating like this for centuries, I can do it for one meal.

If you are the least bit squeamish, don't ask what the item is until after you have eaten it.

◊ Send your host a written thank-you. Acknowledge the special hospitality that has been shown to you by writing your host a note as soon as the very next day. You may want to deliver it yourself or have it delivered with an appropriate gift of flowers. Find out what is customary.

Gift-Giving

Gift-giving in international business can be one of the most perplexing and challenging aspects of your global travels. What you select, when you give it and how you present it are all factors to be carefully considered. You can significantly enhance or totally ruin a business relationship by the simple act of gift-giving. Follow the advice of George Bernard Shaw, "Do not do unto others as you would that they should do unto you. They may not have the same tastes." It is not just a matter of taste when traveling abroad. Culture and custom should also guide gift-giving.

The best gifts are usually ones that reflect your business or the region where you live. The gift should have some meaning for the recipient. Products that are unique to your area like special foods or books about your city are well received, but a CD of your favorite rock star may be meaningless. Since this is about business, accessories for the office make good gifts.

If you choose to give something that reflects your business, consider whether an item with your company logo will appear too aggressive or self-serving.

Know which ones of your international customers appreciate fine gifts and which ones find expensive gifts inappropriate. The English do not exchange gifts in business except at holiday time and then give only moderately priced items. In Germany, gift-giving is not a frequent occurrence. When you do so, choose inexpensive gifts. An expensive gift may be misunderstood and taken for a bribe. However, when you are dealing with the Italians, they are generous and appreciate gifts of quality. The French exchange gifts in business after a relationship has been established, but prefer items that reflect the personal interests of the recipient. In Japan where gift-giving is an important part of doing business, souvenirs of your own city are appealing. As a rule in Asian countries, gift-giving is a common practice. Not bringing gifts to exchange could have a negative effect on your business relations.

The way gifts are received varies from country to country. Don't be disappointed if your international counterpart does not immediately open the gift. In many Asian countries, it is considered rude to open the gift in the presence of the donor. For that reason, you should wait to open a gift in private. As always, follow the lead of your host. When exchanging business gifts in Italy, where so much pleasure is derived from the practice, you would definitely want to open your gift as soon as you receive it.

Check local customs and traditions before you select a gift. Lack of sensitivity to the culture can cost you business. In India you would never want to give a gift made of cowhide since the Hindus consider cows sacred. If you are dealing with Muslims, avoid anything to do with alcohol, pigs or dogs. In Hong Kong giving a clock is bad luck since the word for clock sounds like "death." Sharp objects like knives and scissors signify severing ties in China as well as in several other countries.

Flowers may seem like a safe gift for most occasions, but be aware of the type of flower, the color and the number you give. Chrysanthemums and lilies are equated with death and funerals. Red roses can send a romantic message when you don't intend it. Sending an odd number of flowers is taboo in France and Spain, and in Germany you want to avoid sending thirteen flowers. In Japan stay away from the number four and multiples of four, which is considered an unlucky number. If your Japanese counterpart is in the hospital, don't send a potted plant. Superstition is that the plant encourages the illness to take deeper root.

Checking with a florist in the host country before sending flowers is a smart move.

The gift you give should be wrapped. Take the time to make your gift attractive; if you don't have the skill to do it, have someone do it for you. Some of us just aren't as talented along those lines as others. An unwrapped gift will send the message that you are careless and don't pay attention to detail. Your Asian counterparts will show as much appreciation for the way the gift is wrapped and presented as they will for the gift itself.

Gifts may be presented before you get down to business or after the meeting has been concluded. In Europe, gifts are more often given at the conclusion of your business. In Japan, gifts are usually exchanged at the first meeting. Find out what is customary.

Don't surprise the Japanese with your gift. If they are not prepared for it and happen not to have a gift for you, they will lose face. Saving face is an important issue for the Japanese people.

Appropriate Conversation

It ought to be very clear by now that whatever you do in all your business relations, prior planning is a must. That goes for making conversation as well. Decide in advance what you will talk about with your international partners. Learn what subjects they like to discuss and find out what topics are inappropriate or offensive.

Common sense and good judgment should be your guide before you speak.

Avoid political issues and discussions of wars, past or present, particularly if your country was in the war and on the other side. It would be unthinkable to talk about World War II with the Germans or the Japanese. You wouldn't want to criticize the political leaders of a host country. Although the English tabloids seem to discuss every move of the Royal Family, your comments should brief and positive.

Learn as much as you can about current events in the country you are visiting by reading publications and watching the news. Know something about their favorite pastimes and signature products.

Have an answer ready for that ever popular question, "What do you think of our country?"

Gestures around the World

Learn about gestures in other cultures so that you avoid sending the wrong message. Gestures don't have universal meaning. The "okay" sign with the index finger and the thumb in a circle is considered rude and vulgar in many countries. In France it means zero or worthless. The "V" or victory sign if done with the palm facing you is another insulting gesture. When you want to beckon someone in Japan, you put your palm down instead of up and wag your fingers toward you. If you haven't done your homework, your hand signals can easily offend the other person. By keeping the use of gestures to a minimum, you can avoid uncomfortable situations. However, there is no substitute for good preparation.

Understand the nuances of making eye contact around the world. North Americans and Europeans hold eye contact longer than others. We interpret good eye contact as a signal that someone is listening. In Asia, India, and parts of Africa, people avoid eye contact so that they can concentrate on what is being said. In Japan expect people to maintain eye contact for only a short period of time.

Punctuality

The concept of time and punctuality varies from country to country. Most North Americans believe in being on time and consider it rude to be kept waiting. Most Northern Europeans are of the same mind, but in Southern Europe, people tend to run late. In Central and South America, appointments are just approximations so be prepared to wait for an hour or even longer. When you are doing business in Asia, you will find that most Asians value punctuality and will even arrive early for a meeting.

The best rule to follow around the world is to be on time yourself, but exercise patience if you are kept waiting. Take along some good reading material.

Meeting and Seating

When you are engaged in meetings internationally, learn the protocol of conducting meetings. Find out how much preliminary conversation is usual, who the persons of importance are, how decisions are made and where people are seated at meetings. In Asian countries, importance is paid to hierarchy and rank. Be sure you honor that tradition. Waiting for guidance, watching and listening will keep you on track with your business partners, but the best insurance against a misstep is to do preliminary investigation for each country that you visit.

Doing business globally provides numerous challenges for the most savvy of business people. If you keep in mind that international etiquette is all about respect and courtesy and if you focus more on the other culture than yours, world travel should be a pleasant and profitable experience.

Your Notes Here

Your Notes Here

Your Notes Here

Conclusion

When all is said and done, manners will make the difference. They will make the difference in whether you get that first good job, that exciting promotion, that sought-after account or that fabulous new client. Manners will make the difference in whether you keep the job, get the next promotion or hold on to the account or the client. Your skills may be top-notch, your expertise beyond question and your product terrific; but if you lack interpersonal skills, nothing else will matter. The way you treat others in business is the key to success.

Business etiquette is very simply about feeling and showing kindness and respect for those around us. It has nothing to do with putting on airs or being snobbish and aloof. It is caring enough to observe certain traditional behaviors and being wise enough to exercise good judgement in an ever-changing world. We show that we care about others when we stop to hold a door, when we offer to help with a heavy package, when we go out of our way to say "thank you," when we dress appropriately for the occasion, when we arrive on time for our appointments and when we do what is right for everyone, not just ourselves.

Many of the rules of manners have to do with seemingly unimportant details. Does it really matter if your shoes aren't shined, if your business card is out of date, if you don't stand up to shake hands, or if you skip the small talk and get right down to business? Every one of those details counts in your quest for success and your search for excellence. If you have any doubt, look around you at the successful people. Note their behavior and you will see that they follow the rules of etiquette and pay attention to the fine points. J.W. Marriott said it best — "It's the little things that make the big things possible."

About the Author

Lydia Ramsey is a leading authority on business etiquette and international protocol. She is the president of Lydia Ramsey Inc., based in Savannah, Georgia. She began her career over thirty tears ago as an etiquette consultant for Rich's of Atlanta. She has worked with corporations, educational institutions and nonprofit organizations as a teacher, trainer and consultant, offering her expertise to thousands of people.

Ms. Ramsey grew up in Augusta, Georgia, received a Bachelor's Degree from Agnes Scott College in Atlanta and pursued graduate studies at both Emory University and the University of Pennsylvania. She is active in a number of professional associations including the American Society of Training and Development. She is a member of the Leadership America Alumnae Association.

Ms. Ramsey writes a weekly business etiquette column for the Savannah Morning News and is the publisher of the Etiquette Edge, a quarterly newsletter.

Ms. Ramsey is available as a keynote speaker, workshop presenter and seminar leader. If you would like to advance your business by having Lydia Ramsey share her expert knowledge of manners in the workplace, contact her at 912-598-9812 or email her at etiquette@lydiaramsey.com. You may write to her at:
P.O. Box 16545,
Savannah, GA 31416.

Order Form

MANNERS THAT SELL:
Adding the Polish that Builds Profits

**Detach and return this order form
with your payment today!**

Manners That Sell - $19.95 x __ book(s) = $_____ +
$5 shipping per book x __book(s)=$__ **Total=$_____**

Select method of payment:

☐ Check enclosed   Check # _____
☐ MasterCard   ☐ Visa

Credit Card #:_____ Exp:__ /__

Signature:_____

Name:_____

Address:_____

City:_____ State:____
Zip:_____

  Mail your order form to: Lydia Ramsey
  Ph:(912)598-9812   PO Box 16545
  etiquette@lydiaramsey.com Savannah, GA 31416